Marriage

How to Rebuild and Grow Love, Intimacy, and Connection

Marriage Help, Relationship Advice and Marriage Advice

only. Every attempt has been made to provide accurate, up to date and reliable complete information. No warranties of any kind are expressed or implied. Readers acknowledge that the author is not engaging in the rendering of legal, financial, medical or professional advice.

By reading this document, the reader agrees that under no circumstances are we responsible for any losses, direct or indirect, which are incurred as a result of the use of information contained within this document, including, but not limited to, —errors, omissions, or inaccuracies.

Table of Contents

Marriage

BONUS

Visithttps://funnelb.leadpages.co/smarter-not-harder-business/ to get free eBooks, weekly tips, and the two free bonuses below when you join my free Ultra Book Club. Upgrade your personal and professional life today.

Free Bonuses:

- Top 10 Productivity Tips & Hacks: Guaranteed to Unlock MASSIVE Amounts of Time, CRUSH Decision Fatigue, and SKYROCKET Your Efficiency *and* Effectiveness .
Visit https://funnelb.leadpages.co/smarter-not-harder-business/

- 23 Health Tips & Hacks to CRUSH Fatigue, Improve Sleep, Boost Sex Drive, and Heal Your Gut Visit https://funnelb.leadpages.co/health-tips-fatigue-sleep-sex/

Introduction

"Till death do us part" – an oft-used phrase that reminds us that we have made a commitment to another person to love, to cherish and to be with that person until the end of our days. But if you think about it, how much of this statement is an actual reflection of what we expect from our marriage? Is it really only death that parts us? In the fast-paced modern world of today, divorce rates are going up at an insanely fast pace. Often, we do not have the time to correct things that add up to making a relationship fail. When we do realize that the marriage is failing, it's often too late to fix anyway.

Worse still are those marriages that exist only on paper. Too many couples feel that the romantic part of their marriage fizzles out just a few years into their becoming married. Familiarity may or may not breed contempt but it certainly allows the partners to take one another for granted. And when you add kids to the mix, the situation between spouses becomes one messy tangle that most people just give up on, instead of trying to fix. It doesn't have to be like that and this book looks at why it becomes stale and how to stop that from happening.

There is no cure all and there is no magic to a successful, perfect relationship – such a thing does not even exist! Marriage, like any other relationship in your life, is just a work in progress; simply because you have made your magical vows to stay together for the rest of your lives, it does not mean that you won't have problems. Given that you are rubbing away the boundaries between each other and then merging your respective, individual lives together, there is sure to be friction and difficulty initially. And once you're past that, you want to ensure that the two of you don't get bored with each other, both inside and outside of the bedroom. The love is there, but the expression and reflection of it can sometimes be the element that is missing.

If you find that your marriage is suffering or fizzling out – you've come to the right place! In this book, you will find tips and ideas on how to reconnect with your spouse and rekindle that fire that made you take that huge step in the first place. Keep in mind that these ideas are not foolproof; each couple is different and you have to find the best course of action that suits *you* as individuals. That said, these strategies could get you started on the right path, make you ask the right questions and give you a place to begin your long journey back to one another. That's all anyone can do but the book is based on experience and is written with the express intent of helping you to stay in your relationship and rekindle the love that you once knew.

The book also deals with the ways in which you can look out for the warning signs that something isn't as good as it should be and helps you to overcome becoming a victim to a failed marriage. Even though you go through so many things together, it shouldn't kill off the romance between you and your partner. It covers what happens when children come into the picture and talks about ways in which you really can re-ignite the fires of passion.

I was talking to a married couple the other day about the longevity of their marriage and what they put it down to. They both smiled at each other and gave each other a mischievous grin. One of the things that they said was essential for a good marriage was the ability to laugh together. When we delved deeper, it wasn't just the ability to find fun in similar things though. They had been through some pretty traumatic experiences during the course of a lifetime together. They had been able to face adversity together and it was perhaps their humor and their ability to confide in each other that had brought them through bad times.

You need to understand that marriage for a lifetime means making promises for times ahead that you don't even know about yet. Your commitment to each other has to take into account the unknown and that's where many marriages fall apart. Faced with this unknown, the couple may not know any other way of dealing with the problems that have arisen. However, if you have fundamental trust in each other and can talk about a wide range of things, chances are that you can muddle through like people in successful marriages do. Sometimes, you need to reignite the love aspect of your marriage. After all, how does someone feel after waking up to the same face after fifty years? The way to look at this aspect is to understand that although the person next to you is 50 years older, so are you. Both of you should be able to grow together, to learn together and to see each other as the object of love that you always were. I sometimes look at my own partner and wonder what it was that I initially fell for. It's normal to question things like this, but it shouldn't lead you to dissatisfaction. It should lead you to knowing that if either of you are becoming unhappy, it means learning something new together to keep the marriage every bit as alive as it was the day that you walked down the aisle.

That's where this book comes in. It is chock full of ideas and advice that will help you all the way through your marriage to make it a place that is not just acceptable to both of you but that makes both of you happy. Lasting happiness is something that everyone strives for and if you think of it in that complex way, you can also see that common sense tells you that keeping two people happy is harder than pleasing yourself. The ideas contained in the book are based upon experience and based upon cases where real life problems have occurred that may be similar to your own problems or which demonstrate ways and means to get beyond a particular type of problem.

Marriage is a wonderful place to be, where two people find happiness under the same roof and are able to sustain that happiness. Is the road going to be bumpy? You can bet your life it will be because people's priorities change and you need to work out what they are and how they can work in conjunction with the changes taking place in the life of your partner. When you do, you will be very glad that you did. Sometimes things are not as one sided as you imagine them to be. It takes two to keep a marriage alive and kicking.

Chapter 1: Marriage as an Institution

"It is not a lack of love, but a lack of friendship that makes unhappy marriages."

Friedrich Nietzsche

If you look back through time, you will see that many things have changed on the marriage scene. In fact, there are all kinds of marriages all over the world that are evolving because things change. For example, before the 2nd World War, women expected a man to court her for a respectable period, but the courtship wasn't as simple as it is these days. The family had to approve of the courtship. Those girls who decided to cross the line of respectability and court regardless of parental consent were usually cut off from the family – especially if the family was one that was rich. Men and women were used as pawns to a certain degree and marriages were not exactly arranged, but made up of two people whose marriage may actually better the position of the family in the eyes of society.

Single mums were unheard of in those days and if a girl got pregnant outside of marriage, she may even have been sent away until the event was over and done with so that the family friends knew nothing of the event. Marriage was a serious business arrangement and once you were actually in it, it was unlikely that you would ever have the opportunity to get out of it. These days, that has changed to some degree although there are still those that see divorce as a scandal. When you look at the figures these days, 59 percent of marriages that take place before the couple have reached their late twenties, end in divorce. That number goes down a little after the age of 27 to 50 percent, but that's half of the people getting married! Isn't that a little worrying?

So what went wrong?

Why are people so prone to leaving a situation that they find to be unsatisfactory instead of working on the relationship? The fact is that many who marry in this day and age don't really understand what a lifetime commitment means. Thus, faced with difficulty, they are unable to continue their relationship. It's easier to walk away. If you were to talk to people from the last two generations, you would find that there is a marked difference in opinion about why marriages fail. Our grandmothers may say that people don't know how to pull together, while people of our parent's generation would say that it's easier to divorce than to go through those rough periods. Divorce is more common these days, so a girl is not stigmatized by it any more – as they would have been 50 years ago.

The fact is that you have come to this book looking for answers and it is hoped that by the end of the book, you will realize that the relationship you are in is worth saving. Yes, there are times when you don't agree. You are two individuals but society today has this image of "soul mates" and although it's a very positive thing to believe that there is a "soul mate" out there for you, the majority of marriages that actually succeed are made up of people who know that's not particularly accurate or even realistic. A marriage is made up of two people who have sufficient devotion to each other to weather all the storms that lie ahead. It's as simple as that. And, believe me – there will be storms.

Other reasons why people may remain married could be because of religious belief. In the Catholic Church, for example, divorce is still frowned upon. The "till death us do part" is said intentionally. It's a commitment for life. There isn't a choice as far as the religion is concerned, and yet there are Catholics who do divorce. There was a comparison done between Catholic divorce figures and non-Catholic divorce figures and what was found was interesting. Whereas 50 percent of the general population may divorce at some stage in their lives, the Catholic figures were a lot lower at 28 percent. What can be learned from this is that joint belief in something can help mold the marriage together. It gives another element to consider when times are rough.

It is also very interesting to look at the institution of marriage in other continents. For example, arranged marriages in India have a failure rate of 4 percent. That's pretty amazing, although those in the western world would argue that these are people who do not have freedom of choice. When asked about this freedom of choice, one Indian lady said that her view of marriage was a very positive one and I further questioned her because of my lack of understanding of this system of marriage:

"I love my parents," she explained. "They love me. I have always been a dutiful daughter. When they chose a husband for me, I knew that the choice would be a wise one – not made by the heart of a silly girl – but made by adults who know what marriage involves. I had the right to say "no" and perhaps am fortunate in that respect, but the man who was chosen for me was the perfect match for my temperament, could provide me with a good home and had good moral fiber." Not all marriages that are arranged work but the percentage is very high. One may argue that women don't get the choice and in some countries brides are taken too young. This is true, though in this book, we are looking at consensual marriage rather than merely marriage that is forced upon people.

If you go across to the other side of the world and look at the figures in other countries, they differ because of the background within those countries. For example, those with very low divorce rates appear to be countries where leaving a marriage would be unthinkable and women have no choice. On the other side of the coin, where choice is available, these differ between 47 percent in the United Kingdom, through to a lower 25 percent in Catholic Italy.

The reason for including this in the book is so that you can see an overview of what's happening in the world. If your marriage appears to be getting stale, you are not alone in those thoughts but there are countries where the mentality of the people is different and where marriages do seem to survive at a higher rate. Perhaps these are people who are more tolerant to life's ups and downs or perhaps it's all about the approach to marriage in the first place.

There are those who say that the institution of marriage is dated though when you feel that amount of love for another human being, you want to commit to them and marriage is the obvious way of doing that. Marriage says it all. It says, "I love you above all others." It says "I want to spend the rest of my life with you." and there is no better way of showing your commitment to another human being. You may even find that you want to carry out another ceremony ten years down the line to re-affirm your vows and those who choose to do this really do give their families confidence that nothing has changed and that the love between the couple remains the same.

One can argue against it saying that people can live together these days so there is no need for formalization of the relationship. However, there is more to it than that. When you are married, you commit yourself to that person but you also cover them under the terms of the law. That person is your spouse. He/she has first entitlement when it comes to making decisions that affect you. That's vital to remember since you may just find yourself in a hospital bed wishing you had made the decision to marry and leaving decisions to be made by your parents, even if you have been with your partner for a set number of years. That commitment is for all time. Yes, there is always the potential of divorce, but the institution of marriage helps to secure the ties and make them final. It legitimizes children and gives them the security that they need. Thus, marriage must be considered as the best way forward when you know that your commitment levels are high enough to take the relationship into the next phase. There is a very interesting quotation from Khalil Gibran on the subject of marriage that is every bit as relevant today as it was when it was written:

"Let there be spaces in your togetherness, and let the winds of the heavens dance between you. Love one another but make not a bond of love: Let it rather be a moving sea between the shores of your souls. Fill each other's cup but drink not from one cup. Give one another of your bread but eat not from the same loaf. Sing and dance together and be joyous, but let each one of you be

alone, even as the strings of a lute are alone though they quiver with the same music. Give your hearts, but not into each other's keeping. For only the hand of Life can contain your hearts. And stand together, yet not too near together: For the pillars of the temple stand apart, and the oak tree and the cypress grow not in each other's shadow."

Khalil Gibran

The institution of marriage may seem daunting to those who are not yet familiar with the certainty it gives to a couple in love. Yes, they will always remain individuals within a marriage and that is something that people forget. A marriage may be a combination of two people, but it's never going to be two people made into one. That's the mistake that too many people make when they think of the institution of marriage. This book will help you to gain a better perspective.

This is where some couples go wrong. They believe themselves to be at one with their partners and what this does is lay a heavy burden on the partner who is believed to be the strongest of the pair. Traditionally, men work out to work and this role suited them because their natural instinct is to be the hunter and provider. The woman, on the other hand, was seen as the emotional one. It was her job to bring up the children and to provide a comfortable home for the family. As these roles have changed over the years, so have attitudes. Strong women with careers may not feel that it is their place to be dependent upon a man. Men who are not afraid of their feminine side may be quite happy to change diapers, but you still need to remember the important element of individuality.

There are many books on marriage that miss this point entirely and if you want to improve you marriage, it's one of the most fundamental rules that are unspoken but that form part of the union between a man and a woman. Each person is an individual and the wellbeing of both will be better catered for if both are able to recognize this.

Takeaways from this chapter:

There are many different types of marriage. Relationships where couples have religion in common are likely to be longer lasting than those where no particular religion is followed. The rate of divorce is high because tolerance of difficult circumstance has been lessened by the ability to divorce. However, if one can follow the rule of allowing each party to be an individual in his/her own right, there is likely to be a more harmonious relationship.

You need to examine why you are unhappy and what is lacking from the relationship, though do not be quick to apportion blame. Often this happens because of the response a party to the marriage gets from his/her counterpart allowing personal feelings to get in the way of objectivity. Thus, read on and work out why the marriage is going wrong, rather than jumping to conclusions and apportioning any blame at all. Blame will come back and bite you and if you really want your marriage to work, it won't help.

Instead, examine what you have. Look at the positive aspects of your marriage instead of the negative ones. He who sees the cup half full will always gain more from any relationship than he who sees the cup as half empty. Optimism rather than pessimism and disbelief works to help you to smooth any rough areas that may occur during the course of your marriage. Your relationship with your partner may seem to weaken at times but within the pages of this book are held many of the secrets that couples use to get their marriages back on track. If you see your own weaknesses and are able to overcome them, you can make your marriage stronger.

Chapter 2: Comparing Then and Now

"You don't bring me flowers anymore"

Barbara Streisand

In the early days of a relationship, the two people within a couple are trying to discover each other. It's the natural way for a relationship to progress. Something inside you tells you that the relationship with this guy or gal is worth putting energy into. There's even a kind of electrical spark to the relationship that makes you drop everything and notice him or her when they come onto the scene. You know this is Mr. or Mrs. Right. When you fall into that state of love, there is a period when little else matters. You both become the focal point of each other's lives. When you are not with him, you want to be with him. When he isn't with you, he keeps checking his phone to see if there is a message. This passionate stage of a relationship is part and parcel of the courting game and it's natural to feel obsessed by it.

It's the kind of stuff that movies are made of. You whisk each other up into this passionate place that no one else shares and when this leads to a long-term relationship such as marriage, the honeymoon period does last for a while. However, the introduction of everyday life together and all the mundanity that this life involves erodes the edges of passion and the relationship becomes what people term as "settled." This is the part of marriage that lovebirds may not have seen as even possible. They see through "rose tinted spectacles" and they may not have thought about how two people living in the same space can get on each other's nerves so much. The bad habits surface. There are the responsibilities that are shared, but couples in love don't see the piles of dirty washing and having to clean toilets as being part and parcel of the relationship. For some, this transition from being in the "throws" of love and then being in a practical relationship is too hard. You must have seen movies where the wife runs home to mom within the first couple of months of the marriage, but there's also a very good side that people may not immediately see. All of the practical things that you share can make you stronger as a couple, rather than make the marriage fall apart. You need to see shared experiences as strengths, even if they are negative experiences. The fact that you got past a negative experience says a lot about your strength as a couple.

Thus when you went into your marriage, you may not have been seeing things realistically. You may have had expectations that are difficult for both of you to stick to and that can make things seem bleak. As the years pass, you may also find that you get this awful sense that this wasn't what you really wanted, but it may be the situation you are in or the lack of shared feelings that makes you feel like that, though these can be brought back into your marriage. You just have to want the marriage to work. Conversely, you see people in their eighties who still feel passion for each other and are proud to show off their spouse to new friends. What do they have that you don't?

This is what this book intends to explore, so that you can survive as a couple and come out of the other side of this bad patch as a stronger couple. Remember, having children adds another dimension to your relationship that you may not have been ready for. Whatever the situation, there are universal ways to get beyond bad times and that's what we are here to explore.

Maybe you have had kids and gone through that awful embarrassment when you don't want the kids to witness your passion. Perhaps you just got accustomed to a lowered expectation of passion. The fact is that life knocks a relationship for six as far as passion goes because it's hard to feel passionate in between changing dirty diapers or cleaning up the other person's mess all of the time. In fact, some marriages fail because neither party makes the effort to keep the passion alive. They just drift apart or carry on living their own independent lives ignoring the difficulties of their spouse because they are oblivious to those difficulties. It's not surprising when you consider all of the pressure put on married couples to pay the bills, to get a day's work done and to provide for children who may be a little more demanding than the purse strings allow.

You may have friends who tell you, "He doesn't buy me flowers anymore." You may have others who believe that they are stuck in relationships that are unsatisfactory and they don't have the energy to move on. There will be yet others who took the bull by the horn and decided it was time for the relationship to end because it was too much like hard work to revive it. When you look at the divorce figures, these back this up and show that half of the marriages will end in divorce for one reason or another. You also have the small percentage of marriages that are able to get beyond difficulties and thrive.

Marriage can go all different ways. If Sally sleeps with Dave's best friend, he isn't going to be likely to want to stay with her. Similarly, if Sally finds Dave in bed with one of their original bridesmaids, it isn't going to go down well. The fact is that sometimes you need to go the extra mile to make the passion last. It's a different kind of passion. The kind of passion that married couples feel even after the passage of time is a mellowed kind of passion that not everyone is ready to accept as being the norm. You can spice it up but many don't even have the enthusiasm to try anymore. That's why it's important that you recognize one thing that may be different with your marriage. The fact that you reading this book means that you want to find solutions, rather than walking away from a marriage that isn't living up to its promise and that's a great thing for you to be doing. It means you have no intention of hurting your partner and are merely looking for solutions to make your marriage work, rather than breaking it up.

You see hearts and flowers, music and love, laugher and understanding on the TV when love is in the air. However, what you don't see is dirty underwear, odd socks, stains on the sofa or piles of dishes in the sink. You also don't see the reality of the fact that she snores or that he does and that one of you has put on weight and takes up more than their fair share of the bed. You don't see the irritation of having the toilet seat left in an open position, the toothpaste tube squeezed from the middle instead of the end or all of the hundreds of things that drive couples to a state of frenzy. You also don't see the weight of responsibility that you may have to face together in an era that is known for people being stressed. It is hard work, but we will try and make some simple sense of it, so that you can put your relationship back on track and enjoy each other's company for the rest of your lives without it becoming a life sentence.

So how do couples actually survive the humdrum?

Some do, some don't. If you have a deep level of understanding between you, then the inner love that you feel and the respect that you develop make you able to laugh at all of the mishaps that happen. You share experiences and grow closer together. You share laughter and are there to help out when the tears fall. It's a deeper kind of love than that shown in the initial stages of a relationship and although it may not surface every day of your lives, you know that it's there. It's the one thing you are completely sure of and that your partner is sure of too, but it doesn't happen by chance. It doesn't happen on its own. It takes two people to develop that depth in a relationship and if your relationship has lost some of its sparkle, you also need to know that it's time to decide which way you want that relationship to go.

Marriage

It takes two to get it to go in the right direction. It takes commitment, understanding and wanting the same thing. That commitment, coupled with love, will help you to weather all the bad stuff and survive as a stronger couple. This book is written for those whose relationship may be somewhat dull, but who still feel that the marriage is worth salvaging. If you don't believe that, close the book now, as it's only written for those whose belief in the power of a strong relationship enables them to change with the times and admit a certain amount of responsibility. Remember that for every sin your partner is guilty of, you will be equally guilty as well. The relationship is made out of two people. One woman who discussed her marriage with me said that she found fault in everything that her husband did. She wanted things done around the house and he never finished what he started. When I asked him about it, he said that he loved doing things around the house and would gladly do it if he were left to it. The mistake that she was making was criticizing him all the way through trying to do things to the extent that he just gave up.

If you can work together toward the same aim and both swallow your pride and stubborn insistence that the marriage is going wrong because of one person, then you are likely to be able to rekindle that love and keep your marriage vibrant and happy. Those that do really appreciate their partnerships and these are marriages that pass the test of time with the same amount of ardor with which they began. In the following chapters, we will give you pointers on how to do this, but sometimes it really does pay to take your mind back to the original person that you fell in love with and ask yourself what it was about that person that captured your heart. A small gesture that shows that you remember this is something that will awaken feelings between the two of you that are known only to you.

If you know, for example, that you loved her simplicity and know from your courtship days that there were special wild flowers that she loved, why not stop in the woods and pick them for her? If you, as a woman, remember a special song that meant a lot to both of you, there's nothing wrong with reminding your loved one that you think about it too. Your loved one may think that everyday life got in the way of that kind of thinking and may not be expecting you to ask him to dance by candlelight. A spontaneous mood changer, this can sometimes spark up those original feelings that you had for each other.

Something you need to remember when you are comparing then and now is that in those days when love was in its infancy, neither of you had the weight of responsibility that you have now. Sometimes, you need to let go of that responsibility for a short while and remember the things that mattered to both of you. Of course, that doesn't mean dropping mortgage payments or doing something irresponsible. It simply means remembering the past and showing your partner that you remember it as well. It could be something as symbolic as a picnic in a field or as mind blowing as going away together to a special place and it doesn't have to cost the earth. When I talked to couples about their special memories, many of these were not costly at all.

"We stayed in an old motel together and it was there that we became a couple," one woman told me and once a year, after 40 years of marriage, they go back to that same room to celebrate their love for one another and by today's standard that's a pretty cheap place to stay. However, for them, it's priceless and forms part of their past together. There may be things that you share with your partner. It doesn't have to be something expensive. It can be a memory, a favorite flower, a favorite passage from a poem or anything that is special to both of you. Take that trip down memory lane and find it because there's no doubt, it will be something that is going to be symbolic to your partner as well.

Enjoying the shared experiences

Shared experiences are valuable within a relationship. Whether these are mundane or life changing, a couple goes through all kinds of experiences during the course of their marriage. It's important to take the good with the bad, but it's also important to realize that even though your loved one seemed very different at the outset of your marriage, there may be reasons for the changes that have occurred over the course of the marriage. For example, childbirth can change a woman's attitude toward life but if her man shares in the responsibilities – mundane or not – he can at least see where her tiredness is coming from and help to share the load.

There are going to be bad times as well as good times and the best thing about being married should be the fact that you can keep each other strong. That means that when one partner is going through bad things, the other can take up the slack and help them toward a stronger period in their lives. Bringing up kids can be hard work and can also mean that there are pressures imposed that would not otherwise be there. Solidarity in all decisions will really help. It doesn't help the wife much if the husband comes home and agrees to unreasonable demands made by the children. In fact, it may even alienate her as she sees that the child is being given preferential treatment.

You cannot expect your loved one to be the same person as he/she always was. Time changes people and before you are too critical about the changes that have happened to your spouse, take a good look in the mirror and realize that you have changed too and that you may not be the prize that you were when you met your loved one. Share the joys. Share the insecurities and share the ups and downs of marriage because these help you to accept changes and to embrace them as part of the lives that you live together. Keep in touch with your partner's interests in life and embrace his/her individualism. When you do, you don't see it buried by responsibility and often this happens in marriage and it's never intentional.

The then is gone and the today that you share will be tomorrow's "then." Make it something worth looking back on because it's sure that you will look back and it's better to have positive things to share together to help to make you stronger in order to face your tomorrows. Laugh together, cry together but stay on the same page of your life as your partner is on because those shared pages are the ones that help to make you stronger, as a couple.

Takeaways from this chapter

We accept that life changes. We get older. We have children and our responsibilities change. The part which may make a marriage go a little off track in when one party to the marriage doesn't make any allowance for these changes. If you criticize your partner, you are taking away his/her confidence and that's not going to help the marriage. If you try to take over and put yourself forward as being "perfect" measured against your partner's imperfections, you are breaking the trust your partner places in you. This means that there will be resentment and often this silent resentment is what causes a marriage to fall apart.

The following words are ones that you need to examine:

- Solidarity
- Trust
- Acceptance

Solidarity means being part of an alliance. You don't show your partner up by arguing in front of friends in a way that is intended to belittle your partner. This takes away solidarity. You discuss what's on your mind instead of letting things fester and become larger problems. For example, if you know that the kids are stopping you from having a great sex life, join together with your partner and come up with solutions, so you can have your sex life back again. Avoiding the issue isn't solidarity. If you have problems and are not discussing them, this leads to misunderstanding. This isn't solidarity. Talk to your partner. Joan and Ian stopped talking over the period of bringing up children. She belittled him to his friends and did not feel it necessary to discuss health problems that were getting in the way of emotional and sexual security. She had a prolapse that stopped her from feeling like being sexy. He thought the rejection was her lack of interest in him. The solidarity helps you to understand each other and see things from the same viewpoint. Even if you disagree on something, you should have enough trust in each other to appreciate that sometimes differences are healthy.

Trust means opening up about your feelings, but never laying blame at your partner's door. You should also avoid doing things that destroy trust. Mocking your partner may take away his/her trust.

Finally, acceptance is essential. You are in fact two human beings and, as such, will have differing opinions. That's healthy as long as you accept that your partner is entitled to his/her opinion and do not try to inflict your own opinion on your partner. That individualism is vital to the equation. Allow your partner to celebrate being who he/she is.

Chapter 3 : Communicating Openly

"Any problem, big or small, within a family, always seems to start with bad communication. Someone isn't listening."

~ Emma Thompson

Marriage is a process, not a destination. Perhaps this is the biggest truth that too many couples tend to forget when they take that plunge; they expect a bed of roses and their *'happily ever after'* almost immediately. What we forget that we are not living a fairytale; we live in the real world, where there are real life problems, from financial troubles to having to cater to our kids' needs. Generic as this piece of advice may sound, remember – do not go into a marriage with the expectation of the white picket fence and a perfect family. It may happen one day, if you work toward it, but it's not going to happen overnight. Anyway, communicating your dream to your partner is one way of solidifying that dream within your partner's heart and mind, so that you are both working toward the same thing with the same level of commitment. Indeed, you may even have that wonderful family house with the picket fence and it may be this that is making you think that marriage is going to be a bed of roses, but bricks and mortar are only part of the picture. The two people that live within that house also have expectations and they may not line up exactly right with each other's hopes and dreams. In fact, it would be rare if they did in the early stages of a marriage.

One lottery winner was telling me that his wife's dream was to live in a country cottage with roses around the doorway. Instead of spending their newfound fortune on extravagance, he surprised his wife by providing that dream that she had always had and that meant more to her than all of the potential homes that he could have bought for double the amount of money. What you do when dreams are realized is validate that not only do you know what your partner's wishes are, but you are also happy to be in the same dream as your partner. Communicating your dreams and wishes over the years really helps you to be on the same page. There are times when marriages split up because those dreams were not understood. Over the course of time, a couple with careers may pull in different directions even if they have the same overall ambition. Elise and her husband did just that. He was offered promotion within another state and saw this as the quick way to give them that dream existence that Elise had always craved. However, what he had not taken into account was that by not sharing his promotion news and by saying "yes" to it before sharing, he had betrayed her trust. She was unwilling to leave all of her friends and family as she saw them as forming part of her dream, rather than being 4 states away. The balancing act is a very fine one and their marriage didn't survive. He saw the dream coming true and grasped it for what he saw as all of the right reasons, without taking account of his wife's need to be with people who were familiar to her. Faced with the prospect of going to another state where she knew no one,

Elise lost her cool. It would probably have worked out better had he confided in her before saying "yes" but by agreeing to the promotion unreservedly, he was making decisions for her life as well as for his own without any form of consultation. This is what she saw as lack of trust. It is important that couples talk about things that matter and do not assume agreement while there has been absolutely no consultation.

Expectations can ruin your marriage. That's not to say that you shouldn't expect your partner to be there for you when you need him/her to be, or pick up the pieces when life throws unexpected hurdles at you. What's important is letting your partner *know* what you expect – clichéd as this is, communication is the most important thing in any relationship, and even more so in a marriage. But it is this communication that most people find hard to keep up. There are only so many things that you can talk about after all. Once you know a person well, how do you find things to say? The trick is that you should never take things for granted. Just because she wanted to have a house with all mod cons ten years ago doesn't mean the dream is the same now. Give her credit for being flexible in her life and for growing in development. Similarly, what he wants out of life will change too. Talk about it. When you see an opportunity to bring up subjects such as this, lay the cards on the table and encourage open discourse. In my marriage, my partner doesn't like cold weather. It is my dream to see the Aurora Borealis but this involves going to a very cold climate. I joked with my partner about this dream and said that part of the dream was not to have a partner next to me, spoiling the whole illusion by complaining about the cold. My partner understood perfectly and bought me a ticket to go, appreciating that it meant a lot to me. Similarly, I know that my spouse wants to go to Tibet and that's fine with me because being in a marriage doesn't mean locking your dreams away. You can still have them. If you have family to cater for, then you may have to wait, but communicating your hopes, dreams and wishes makes them known and it is then that possibilities may just arise.

So in this chapter, what I am going to do is help you communicate better with your partner. It will not be easy, though it sounds so in theory; letting go of our personal inhibitions can be hard, especially when it comes to bringing down our barriers in front of the person we trust the most. But be patient, and let yourself work through it – you will be able to get there eventually. (That's the second thing you must remember – *being patient*. It takes time to reconnect; you can't expect to go from not talking to one another to jumping into sharing everything in the space of one week).

To begin with, let us do a relationship autopsy. Take your relationship with your partner and look at it from these angles to figure out why you feel so off with the whole issue. It will help you identify where you are going wrong – if you are at all – and then take measures to correct it. Here are a few questions you can ask to dissect your relationship. Answer them honestly. There's no point in skimming over them and deciding that everything is okay between you, when clearly it is not. You came to read this book because you want answers and the only way you can glean them is to take the subject seriously and give it the consideration it merits.

What are your problems with the relationship? Why are you frustrated?
What are your expectations from the relationship? Is your partner meeting them? Does he/she know about them?
What is it about your partner that irritates/upsets you?
Do you know the problems with you that your partner gets annoyed about?
Have you done anything that warrants any kind of ignorance from your partner?
Did you have to change yourself to please your partner? If so, then in what way?
Do you want your partner to change for you? If so, in what way?
When you and your partner talk, what do you talk about? What did you used to talk about, before you were married?
What don't you talk about?

Answer these questions and take the time to write down the answers and you will be able to find out where the problem lies. Writing them down helps you to face up to the problems as being real. In fact, it affirms them and enables you to see them in a clearer light. More often than not, you will find that communication is the key to being able to understand yourself and your partner – but that communication is the hardest thing of all to do once any problem occurs. The problem lies with the fact that we don't know how to handle conflict with one another, and instead of hashing it out together, we end up fighting.

Let us look at an example. Deanna is upset with her husband Casper for leaving his socks around the house when he gets home from work and changes his clothing.

But instead of just telling him about it, she drops passive aggressive comments on his habits, trying to package her problem with him into a simple joke or a sexist comment about men's laziness. She doesn't want to confront him directly – she expects that he understands where she is coming from and will change all by himself. In the end, all that happens is that Casper gets annoyed with her constant 'nagging' and they end up fighting or giving each other the cold shoulder.

The problem is that both Deanna and Casper approach the conflict like they are on opposite sides, with one of them having to emerge the victor. What they forget is that marriage is *not* a contest; one person does not win because the other gives in. This approach leaves both feeling like their partner doesn't understand them at all – did they marry the wrong person then?

There is one more possibility. If Deanna wants to avoid the confrontation and thinks his behavior will improve over time, she will end up pretending this behavior doesn't exist at all. Neither Casper nor Deanna acknowledge the fact that there is a problem – even something as small as this – and this avoidance will lead to unresolved conflicts and it will blow up into something bigger later. The wounds fester, resentment builds up and then the inevitable blow out comes. It would have been better if she had been straight about it and told him that it isn't acceptable to expect her to clean up after him. When you feel something, stop hiding behind little jokes and hints because these don't help things at all. Make your feelings clear because men need clarity. I remember my mother being upset at my father for leaving tea mugs lying around the house. She would make snide comments about there not being any mugs left in the kitchen and he never took the hint. I suggested to her that she tell him straight and she surprised him and me by doing that in no uncertain terms:

"If you want a cup of coffee out of me, then you had better bring me all the cups that you have left all over the house because I am not going looking for them."

To her surprise, he was very compliant and as he knew that only he would suffer if he continued, he soon stopped the habit. He was actually taken aback by her comment and it hit the right chord with him. Sometimes being straight is the only way to be. Had Deanna been straight with her husband, she could have told him that his clothing would remain on the floor and that when he wanted clean clothes, he wouldn't find them because she refused to pick up his dirty clothes after him.

Resolve your issues right then and there. Tell your partner what the problem is and be open about it, instead of trying to make your partner feel like he/she is making a mistake and should therefore try to make it up to you. Be honest instead of patronizing. Deanna could, for example, show him how annoying it is to have clothing all over the floor and say to him that she is grateful that it's only his socks. That makes him aware that there is a problem and he may even be more conscious about fixing it. Similarly, if she does something that irks him, he can find a kind way of addressing it that doesn't really pass off blame. Supposing she spent hours on the phone with her friends and ignored him. He could suggest they do something together that takes her away from the phone. Chances are that she needs her friends to make up for the actual fact that her husband doesn't talk to her any more.

Marriage

Of course, this kind of open communication is easier said than done. More often than not, we end up shooting our mouths off and saying the wrong thing, even when we don't mean it. It's hard to be that open and vulnerable to someone else, even if it is the person we have chosen to spend the rest of our lives with. The love is there, but so are the anger and the resentment and if you let it build up, that resentment can kill a relationship.

So here is a simple way of getting rid of it. This is an easy exercise that couples can perform to help them communicate better with each other. It takes exactly two minutes in a day and if you do it daily, or at least 3-4 times a week, I guarantee that your relationship will improve.

To make it simple to understand, I will use the example of Deanna and Casper once again. Both of them must sit together, on the couch or even the bed, facing the same direction such that one is behind the other. For this instance, let us say that Deanna is the person sitting behind Casper – she must reach out and wrap her arms around his waist and hold him to her.

Given that Casper is the one being held, it is his turn to speak. For the next two minutes, he speaks uninterrupted; Deanna must *not* respond to him in any way, except to simply hold him close. He can tell her anything he wants, whether it is communicating the problem – the 'nagging' in this situation – or even something nice, like a funny thing that happened during the day. The point is to tell her what he thinks, uninterrupted and without any hesitation. If you don't feel like talking, then that is also okay, provided that you sit together for the entire two minutes and just relax into one another.

Once the two minutes are over, neither Deanna nor Casper can talk about those words shared. Whatever Casper spoke to her about is *not* something she can respond to – she must only listen. Also keep in mind that you shouldn't exceed your two minutes. Keep it short; keep it simple.

Now the next evening, switch. It is Casper's turn to hold Deanna as she uses her two minutes to tell him what's on her mind or even sit in silence. Again, Casper *cannot* respond to her and must simply let her speak. After the two minutes are over, neither of them speak about it.

And the cardinal rule – this is *not* foreplay for sex! This is a method of communicating with one another, not meant to lead to bedroom shenanigans. We have entire chapter dedicated to reconnecting between the sheets later, so you can check that out for sexy times – right now, focus on being able to let your partner know what you think and what you feel. It may be a good idea to stick to the couch for this exercise if you feel you won't be able to hold back from making love.

Do this 2-3 times a week and take turns to do it. Make sure both of you evenly split the chances to speak – flip a coin for the first time so that it doesn't lead to yet another conflict between you.

The reason this works is very simple. It's easy being honest with someone whose face you cannot see – so when Deanna is sitting behind Casper, he is far less afraid to tell her what he really thinks. Given that she also cannot respond to what he wants to say, the fear of confrontation – which leads to avoidance and/or resentment – is also negated, allowing him to speak his mind freely, without worrying about judgment or conflict. If he spoke to

Deanna normally, outside of this exercise, she would probably defend herself and the issue would disintegrate into a fight, where both parties cling to their sides and refuse to budge. This way, however, the problem is out in the open and they both can begin to do something about it. There is a captive audience invested in just listening and not talking back.

Given the no feedback rule, Casper must clamp down on the urge to defend his position or respond to Deanna in any manner. The righteous indignation has no place in their relationship anymore; he *can't* respond to the issue verbally, so he begins to consider his behavior to see if anything can be done. So if Deanna says that her problem lies with his nature as a slob, he will begin to try to keep things a bit cleaner and that will definitely make his wife happy.

What this exercise does is ensure you of your partner's undivided attention. It is simple, it is easy and it isn't really anything new – just like your marriage itself. It helps you reconnect with one another on a personal level that you have lost over time. Given that there is no fear of judgment, conflict or even a reaction, you are free to say what you really think, which is what open communication is all about.

Remember – it doesn't always have to be an issue you're discussing! You can simply sit for an entire two minutes together in silence; you could talk about the kids, the gravitation pulls of the moon over the tides, or even list out the ingredients for dinner tonight. The point is to sit together for two minutes and lean on each other.

The other reason why this works so well is the physical touch aspect of it. Modern society has, in rather subtle ways, classified touch as a hedonistic approach to life; reaching out for one another and cuddling is always reserved for either before or after sex. However, science has proved that just plain physical contact with another human being is soothing and calming; it doesn't have to be sexual or passionate. Doesn't it feel wonderful to be held by your partner, without any expectations whatsoever?

So how do you introduce this into your marital routine? You could say that you picked the idea up from a book or from TV and want to give it a go. Make sure that both of you know the ground rules. Let's face it; if your relationship has hit the doldrums, he will be happy to comply with it to see where it goes. He may even get to look forward to this part of your daily routine together.

And so, we move into our second exercise of the day. Now this is not so much an exercise as it is a principle – the principle of physical touch. Given that you have been practicing the previous exercise for a while now, you've probably managed to open the communication channel up to a certain extent between the two of you. So the next time you sit down to have a discussion that you know will dissolve into a conflict, make sure you're touching each other.

Take special note over the course of the next one-week. You don't have to do anything special; just make a diary of all the times you and your spouse were touching and how you felt about it. When you fight, you will notice that, inevitably, the two of you move away from one another. You do *not* touch, not unless one of you has aggressive tendencies and you raise a hand to hit them, in which case, the point is moot – that's abuse.

But touching one another with softness or tenderness isn't something that you associate with anger and argument. So the next time you find your discussion dissolving into a fight, pull your partner close and just touch them gently – the touch becomes a physical, lasting reminder of the fact that the relationship is more important than winning the argument. It grounds you and allows you to regroup. Quickly perform the previous exercise next so that you know what the issue is. Once you have it out in the open, you can begin to resolve it together.

Now another issue that a lot of couples face is being misunderstood. The first exercise is definitely a brilliant way to overcome that, but there is another method called *mirroring* that you can take up to make sure your partners truly comprehends what you are saying.

Most often, when you're fighting and throw out hurtful statements, the phrase you hear is *'What do you mean by that?'* Miscommunication and misunderstandings can ruin a relationship – mirroring is an excellent way to end this cross-connection. Remember though, that it really doesn't help to do it in the middle of a fight. Stop, calm down and then speak to your partner in a non-confrontational manner.

Mirroring is essentially repeating what your partner said to you. For instance, if Deanna screams at Casper that she hates his nature as a slob, Casper, instead of reacting to her, spends some time calming both of them down – preferably with his touch – and then speaks to her rationally. He asks her *"Are you saying that you hate me throwing my socks around?"*

What he is doing is clearing up any misunderstanding in their communication; he is trying to understand where his wife is coming from. Now the important thing here, is to be open to what she responds to him with – he must not get angry if she says yes or no. Or rather, he shouldn't react to her in an angry fashion – that is just going to lead to more conflict. It may hurt, it may be painful, but if he makes sure he *understands* what she wants from him, they can begin to work towards rebuilding the trust.

More often than not, what we say gets lost in translation. Even in an open communication channel, what we say may or may not be what the other person understands fully. Mirroring allows you to repeat to them what you have understood and lets them know if you are on the right track. The point of mirroring is not to defend yourself or not to be right – it is to understand the extent to which your partner understands you and where you may or may not be going wrong.

How you argue and how you end that argument makes all the difference. Too often, fights end up being more about control and winning than truly resolving a conflict. We end up being self-righteous and indignant, and the combination of the two leaves our relationship in dire streets. Now keep in mind the following tips the next time you have an argument with your significant other. Arguments will happen – that's part of marriage – but if you can keep it to certain parameters, you can control the eventual fallout and make sure your marriage doesn't take a hit.

- Keep it private. The whole world doesn't need to know about your fights; you're going to embarrass yourself and your partner if you scream at them publicly and that will lead to more resentment. Also, kids are quite sensitive to their parents' arguments; if you fight in front of them, they will be emotionally affected. Prolonged exposure to their parents' fights can scar them mentally to the extent that they may even need therapy to get through it. So take it to the bedroom and work out your issues quietly.

- Be relevant. The tendency is to drag up ages-old history to fling at your partner when you're fighting. What you're looking to do is lash out and hurt your spouse, not resolve the conflict. Keep to the matter at hand and be relevant – let bygones be bygones.

- Retreat from the argument with dignity or allow your partner to do so. How you end the fight is critical; you can go to bed alone or cuddle together in relief. Be open to the olive branch that your partner extends in the form of a joke or an apology and just let it go.

- Once the argument is over, just let it vanish from your life. Don't let the resentment stretch on indefinitely – if it does, then it's possible you never got to discuss the root of the problem, only its symptoms. Identify the root and hash that out; once it's over, let it be over.

Above all, keep in mind that talking to your partner makes all the difference. And when you talk, don't just discuss the weather, the kids or the family finances. Try to have conversations the way you used to – about your interests, your hobbies and the like. Take the time to *listen* and enjoy one another like you used to.

Communication is key to all relationships and when you are close up and personal with another human being, such as in a marital relationship, you need to keep these channels open and be able to discuss anything and everything. If there are thing that you feel have been left that need to be said, keep a diary of them and let them out when you have your next talk together.

You have to appreciate that if you are unhappy within your marriage, then your partner is unhappy too. The way that you act toward your partner will show your level of unhappiness and that can only result in more unhappiness. In the next chapter, we are going to tackle this a little further with some suggestions about how to keep your independence even when you are married.

Although you may think that promising your life to someone means giving up your independence, there are several reasons why you shouldn't be too fast to give into being an extension of someone else. Two individuals came into the marriage and they should still be there, no matter how many years have gone by or how many experiences you have shared. People who communicate openly and who retain their independent nature can really look forward to years and years of happy marriage without the compromise of losing identity. It is that identity that brought you together in the first place – so hold onto it and don't let marriage drown it.

Takeaways from this chapter

We know that confrontation is not useful. Therefore, the two exercises that have been introduced in this chapter help you to overcome confrontation and replace it with communication. The first exercise was one that involved touch and communication at the same time. If you are able to be that close to your partner and address your worries, chances are that your partner will be more understanding.

It is wrong to assume that you can speak for your partner. For example, if you are invited to dinner with friends, ask your partner if he/she is available that day and whether he/she would like to go. What you are doing is reaffirming that you respect your partner's opinion instead of taking your partner for granted. If you want to invite people over to the house, ask your partner when would be a good time. You do need to work on these aspects of communication and overcome what is essentially making your marriage unhappy. Here are the key things that you need to remember if you want your marriage to be happy:

1. The partnership is made up of two people who both have opinions
2. The couple need to share opinions regularly
3. The couple needs to share frustrations as well but there should be no consequence other than a positive one.
4. One partner should never take the other for granted.

5. You need to avoid confrontation and find a new way to overcome difficulties.
6. Equal respect is vital to make your relationship work.

If you can remember these 6 rules, you will find that your communication becomes more pleasurable because you know that your partner is going to listen to you. You also know that your partner respects you sufficiently to allow you to voice your opinion. Just as you are permitted to voice your opinion, your partner should also be given that freedom of expression without having to dread consequence. Only you can make that happen.

If your reaction is brusque and thoughtless, the chances of getting back onto a good footing are lessened. Thus, before retorting to a comment made by your partner, give yourself sufficient space to think through a thoughtful answer. Even if that means saying, "I need a little time to think about this..." you are leaving the pathway to some kind of discourse open. If you reply in haste and in a negative fashion, you close the door firmly and lose the opportunity of sharing something important with your partner. That serves very little purpose either in the long term or short term.

Chapter 4: Differing Opinions Are Healthy

"My opinions may have changed, but not the fact that I'm right."

Ashleigh Brilliant

The above quotation is very much "tongue in cheek" but opinions are something that married people are entitled to have and those opinions do not have to have the same unity as the marriage does. In fact, it's healthy to have different opinions because when you join two people together with differing opinions, both learn from one another. In an instance many years ago, I remember a couple that were very close to each other arguing about politics at a party. Others around them assumed them to be having an argument. I remember hearing the murmur that their marriage must be in trouble. I laughed at the thought as I knew the couple well and they were one of the happiest couples I had ever met. What they had agreed upon was that even though they were a couple, there was no reason on Earth why their opinions should become docile or mirror one another. Both were intelligent human beings with opinions that were backed up by their experience and they had a right to differ in what they believed.

If you look at some couples, these opinions seem to be stifled. He will watch the same programs on the TV as she wants to watch or vice versa. She will put up with his friends even though she doesn't like them much. But what these couples are refusing to see is that it doesn't have to be that way. People are entitled to their own opinions and opinions can be very good fun when discussed. Someone of one persuasion can give a really interesting talk to another who believes in different things and as long as there is mutual respect for one another, there is no loss and in fact, much to be gained from being free to speak one's mind.

Unfortunately, some believe that when marriage happens, the differences stop and that's sad because stifled opinions can cause a great deal of tension and resentment down the line. Take for example, my partner and me. My partner would love to own a VW camper and go off across the country in a Bohemian way. However, I am the realist. Not only would he find that the camper would give him back ache, but I do not really enjoy the idea of sleeping, eating and performing my toiletry needs in the space provided by a camper. He argues that you can cook outside. I argue that it won't stop the condensation from happening on the windows overnight or the stale smell of bodies squashed into a small space. We both have opinions and we actually find it quite a sport allowing our opinions to be known. He will argue that he could go off in the camper on his own and I say that perhaps he could drop me at a nearby hotel. We both want different things, but neither one of us would impose those things on their partner, knowing that they are opposed to our ideas.

If you are honest about your opinions, this helps the relationship to evolve. I can cite a case here that demonstrates how bad it is to assume that your partner thinks in the same way as you do. In this particular case, my mother assumed that my father enjoyed eating "Turkish Delight." He had never told her otherwise and every birthday and Christmas, she would tell all of us to get father some "Turkish Delight." When she died, I remember my father, as a very old man, joking with us about "Turkish Delight" and telling us never to buy it for him again because he detested it. In this case, the deception wasn't serious enough to make the relationship suffer but in many cases it is. A woman pretends that she likes something, when in fact she detests it. A man may give all the signals that he enjoys something he detests. When you do that in marriage, you build up a kind of resentment because the person on the receiving end is always going to be frustrated at having to do as his/her partner dictates. It's not a dictatorship. It's a marriage of minds and that means that each of you has an opinion and has the right to voice it.

There is nothing healthier than airing your views and being open to listening to your partner's views. What you are doing is learning to understand how your partner ticks without taking for granted that you already know. A difference of opinion is very healthy indeed and shows that you have a mind of your own and that you don't need someone else's opinion rammed down your throat. When asked how she was going to vote, Shirley was fast to tell her husband that her vote was private. He laughed to himself but was never led to assume that she would vote any other way than the way that her conscience told her to vote. Conversely you have couples that live in a false sense of security and then say things like "I have always voted this way because my husband does." That shows narrow mindedness at best and certainly doesn't give anyone confidence in the vote that has been cast.

You have to remember that you are an individual and it's very important that you always remain one. You are not an extension of your partner. He/she is not an extension of you. Just as you should expect to have your own opinions, it's important that you respect that your partner also has that prerogative. We try to teach children to be independent thinkers and yet settle for less in our own home territory and that's a huge mistake. There's a difference between having a difference of opinion and being obnoxious about it. As long as you respect your partner's right to have his/her own opinion, you should expect nothing less from your partner. If you find that your partner is not affording you that amount of respect, then it's time to make your position clear and let him/her know that you don't take kindly to having your opinion dictated to you. There is no need for rudeness or impoliteness. Simply state what you believe so that your partner knows who you are, rather than who your partner assumes you to be. Keep your self-esteem intact and by the same token, appreciate that your partner has opinions that differ from yours.

Takeaways from this chapter

We have learned in this chapter that differences of opinion are normal. Thus, if you find yourself questioning why you are going along with what your spouse wants, you need to appreciate that you are both individuals and perhaps want different things. That doesn't mean you are not compatible. It just means that you are acknowledging your individuality. If you find that you are doing things to please your partner that do not please you very much, it's time to be honest about it because people who are unsatisfied in their lives are often unhappy or this seeming incompatibility can get in the way of enjoying your relationship.

Thus following the rules set out below, you can have your cake and eat it. You are not your partner. Don't try to be:

1. Allow your partner to follow his/her passions without expecting them to be yours.
2. Appreciate and encourage your partner in his/her pursuits.
3. Find space when your compatibilities differ.
4. Enjoy your hobbies and interests without inflicting them on your partner.
5. Don't let your partner inflict his/her interests on you but acknowledge the validity of those interests.

If you can follow those guidelines, you will find that you can live in harmony and have less differences of opinion. Thus, if he wants a night in watching sports with his friends and this is not of interest to you, use the opportunity to get together with the girls for an evening that may not interest him.

You can see from this chapter that a difference of opinions or interests should not deter you from getting on well with your partner, provided that there are reasonable boundaries. For example, if he wants to spend every evening with his pals, this may be conflicting because it's not giving his wife sufficient family time. These are the conflicts that need to be talked about. The catchword is compromise. Finding a compromise is like moving forward with a positive attitude, knowing that both of you respect each other and are able to discuss differences calmly.

It is this calm discussion and support for one another that make a marriage more interesting. You may find that your partner's hobby becomes yours but it should be your choice, rather than obligation. When you find that balance, your married life will become much more harmonious and happy. Enjoy being you and allow your partner to enjoy being him/herself, without harnessing their enthusiasm for the things your partner feels are important.

Chapter 5: Learning to Cohabit

"Women who say that they have met the most amazing guy in the world are only saying that because they haven't lived with them yet."

– Heather Chapple

When you first get together, you don't see the reality of living together. You see this as some magical thing where two lovers will share the same space. It is not as simple as that, as you have probably found out. There are tasks to do. There is the running of the household that needs to be dealt with, the everyday finances and also the routine. Learning to live in the same space as someone else isn't very easy to do. You may have idealized views about how it will go, but believe me, until you actually do it, you don't know what lies ahead in the way of mundanity. You will argue over small things, as we have previously shown you, but you will also question why you are sharing things with your partner when you are accustomed to doing these for yourself.

Unfortunately, one of the biggest mistakes that couples can make is trying to be natural about it when it fact there's nothing natural at all about living under the same roof as someone else. A woman is naturally a care giving person. A man is naturally the hunter. Thus, how can two totally different people find some kind of peace within their lives together, when they both think so differently? The fact is that some couples manage very well indeed, while others find that they struggle. So what's the difference? The main difference is the ability to adapt and adaptation is what it's all about.

If you are a two-car family, then you can probably find some easy way to entwine your lives without too much difficulty as far as going to work is concerned. However, if you only have one car between you, you need to work out a routine so that both parties have their needs catered for. The things that you do need to look at which will cause problems within the marriage as far as cohabitation is concerned are these:

- How will you work your routines out to suit your partner?

- What time will mealtimes happen?

- Who will do the cooking?

- Who will do the housework?

- Who gets up early and who doesn't?

There's a lot more than that to ask, but it's as well to know your partner pretty well. Let's start with an average day. Who gets up early? How noisy is that person? Imagine someone who has worked the night shift at the hospital and who comes home for their sleep being noisily woken up by their partner's thoughtlessness. That was the biggest bugbear that Janet had to face. Her husband's routine was such that he got out of bed early in the morning and went straight into music mode. It wasn't just the music. It was the volume. She suddenly found herself in a world that was noisy and she was unable to get the sleep that she needed. Even hinting about it didn't work. In the end, in a moment of real anger, she stormed into the living room and pulled the socket from the stereo out of the wall. Such was her ire. If you have different timetables and different likes and dislikes, you really have to discuss them so that you can both respect the parameters set by your partner or with your partner. In this case, Janet needed that sleep. It wasn't something she was being particularly difficult about, but it did mean that her husband needed to be more considerate in the mornings.

Then you have people who work at home. Kelly is a writer. She takes her work very seriously and works between the hours of 9 until 12 every day. Unfortunately, since her husband doesn't work until lunchtime, he tends to fight to get her attention during what she sees as her working time. He makes a lot of noise and distracts her and doesn't realize the significance that this has on her work. One could argue that she could have adjusted her hours so that she spent more time with her husband and that's what she eventually did. When you are going to move in together, you have to set boundaries so that both of you know what the score is and do not upset the whole applecart for your partner. It can be enough to split the relationship. The rules that you make between you for cohabiting should include:

- Who works when?

- What privacy is required?

- What kind of music you both like?

- When it needs to be listened to with a headset

- When sleep is needed

- How your work hours affect your home life

Getting things like this straightened out before you actually get together can save you a lot of heartbreak but if you find that your partner is not respecting any of the parameters that you need to be in your life, you need to sit down and talk about it.

Setting up boundaries

If a man needs his wife to be available for dinner parties because of work, then he needs to let her know in advance and discuss the kind of people she will be expected to cater for. That's only fair. Springing this onto a woman at the last minute isn't acceptable. In fact, it shows little consideration since a woman not only has to shop for the event, but has to plan it around her schedule as well.

Similarly, if a woman needs her husband to respect her parameters for work time, she needs to let him know. It's actually better if she has a space that is designated for work where she can close the doors and keep him out but this isn't always practical in this day and age and talking about it will help him to understand that she does need that peace and quiet in order to achieve her work.

Who does the cooking? – This can be discussed between a couple and even if you have been in a relationship for a while, you may be surprised that your partner is actually open to doing a bit of cooking but may have been made to feel that you feel it's your territory. Don't be territorial and try to share the duty because you may find your husband is a better cook than you!

Who does the cleaning? – These are things that can really get in the way of a good marriage. If there is no agreement between you, you will start to see things slip. No one wants to clean the toilet, the bed gets left unmade and eventually it will wear you down. You need to work this out between you at the beginning and stick to a plan. You can actually get away with minimal cleaning if you try to stick to the rule that when you leave a room, you leave it clean and ready for the next day. That means making the bed in the morning, clearing up the dishes after a meal and generally keeping the house looking nice.

Who pays for what? – This is something that has the potential of causing huge arguments in the future if you don't sort it out now. If you are both earning, why not have a joint account and let one of you reconcile that account once a month, letting the other know how much is left to spend? However, if there is only one person earning, this can cause difficulties. You need to decide in advance how you will handle finances so that there are no arguments down the line about who is spending what.

Bad habits – It's not a bad idea to sit down and talk about your bad habits occasionally and learn what your partner feels your bad habits are. For example, do you clean the bathtub after you use it? How about keeping the top on the toothpaste tube? Talk about your bad habits and thrash out ways that you can stem them to make them work with your partner's bad habits. No one on this Earth is perfect and you are both grown up enough to realize that. I remember my father telling me all about my mom's bad habit of collecting things and it was something I began to recognize in myself. They joked about it, but there came a point when it became a problem. If you allow your little bad habits to grow, it can be a lot harder to deal with them at a later stage. In my mother's case, the house was crowded out with stuff and it was only when they moved into a smaller retirement house that she realized how out of control her habit was. Talk about your quirks and learn about those of your partner.

Takeaways from this chapter

Cohabiting is the reality. When you think in advance about all of the perks of marriage, often you don't see the disadvantages and they can creep up on you. If you find that you haven't really sorted out the things that need to be sorted out, then now is the time to sit down with your partner and work out who is responsible for what. It isn't the same as in the old days any more. Women form a huge part of the workforce and even if they are working from home, that work needs to be taken seriously especially if it is contributing toward the family finances. You need to remember that there are two points of view and that you won't agree on everything. That's because you were both brought up in different ways. Perhaps your wife is accustomed to her mother having help with domestic duties and she finds it hard to cope. Perhaps your husband is accustomed to being the only one who brings in the money.

Only you can decide what applies to your marriage. However, you do need to discuss the following:

1. What things in your everyday life upset you and how can they be solved?
2. Is it possible that you can swap certain roles?
3. Are you able to cohabit and respect each other's needs or work space?
4. What leisure time do you need and are you getting it?

By discussing these cohabitation issues, you are able to get things off on the right track. Husbands and wives are not each other's slaves. However, you also need to remember that the sharing of chores should be something that has divisions, so that each of you know who does what. For example, taking the garbage out may be his contribution to cleaning up. It's a small gesture, but one that can go a long way to help keep the house in order. By each of you appreciating the tasks of each other, you learn to cohabit in a happier way and appreciate what your partner does for you. Your partner, in turn, learns to appreciate you. Swap tasks from time to time so that you are both aware of how much work your partner puts into the cohabitation. Empathy, or being able to step into your partner's shoes, helps you to become a lot more appreciative of the other side of the coin and that is valuable in any relationship.

You will also learn a lot more about your partner when you cohabit and your partner may have strengths you were unaware of. Your partner may love to cook and to create great meals for friends and family. Don't stifle that creativity by thinking that certain roles are for a woman and others for a man. There are traditional roles within society, but times are changing and it is acceptable that you choose your own roles based on your own personal strengths and weaknesses.

Chapter 6: The Importance of Independence

"Be who you are and say what you feel, because those who mind don't matter, and those who matter don't mind."

– Bernard Baruch

When you met your loved one and fell in love, you kind of loved him/ her for who he/ she was. That is an individual. When you join together and get married, sometimes that individuality gets lost somewhere under the weight of responsibilities to each other, to children and to keeping life going. It's hard work getting all of the money together to make life work. It is also stressful. The weight of responsibility of marriage can be an enormous weight and you work together to have whatever it is that you need, but forget all about the importance of being yourself.

Let's take a case scenario that may seem a little extreme but it's not. It's actual fact. Mary and Jim were married for forty years. Because he was a very strong character, he insisted on dealing with everything. He paid the bills, he kept the checkbook, he drove the car even though she did have a driving license and when he died of a heart attack, Mary was suddenly left feeling totally useless. She had no idea how much money was in the bank. She had no idea what the house cost to run. This may seem extreme but what happens if one party to the marriage is stronger than the other is that in the case of emergency, the weaker party is less able to cope. Would he have wanted her to struggle so hard? Of course not, but he felt that he was protecting her. When talking to her several years later, she confided that there was a certain resentment within her because there were many dreams that she had that he would never have considered a possibility. Because she loved him, she went along with his ideas of what was right and what was wrong. That's not the way for a really successful marriage to work at all.

Each person needs to feel like an equal in a marriage. Look at your own marriage. If you take the lead in everything, how can your partner actually feel good about him/herself? Jane worked hard all her life but she did so at the expense of her relationship because she tried to control everything. Her husband felt very much as if he was useless and lost self-esteem along the way because she was the only one contributing to the financial side of the marriage. If you were to go back a few years, her husband had a very successful job and loved it, but injury got in the way.

What you need to be aware of is that change happens and if you want to avoid the conflict getting into your relationship, you need to be able to allow your partner the independence that he/she had when you were first together, so that everyone gets to do the things that they want to do and if the worst case scenario happens, they are capable of sorting life out for themselves.

There are other reasons why independence is so important. If a woman puts off the dreams that she has in life to bring up children, she is likely to feel resentment at a later time because she was never allowed to do the things she wanted to do. If a man has to work every day of his life to keep up with the responsibility of keeping his home, then it's not fair on him either. He should have time to do the things that he wants to do.

Therefore, you need to strike the balance somewhere. This helps your partner become the person that he/she was when you were first together. Suppose she enjoys line dancing and wants to go to classes, then there's no reason why they can't arrange that she is allowed to go. If that means getting a babysitter in, for example, then that's what needs to be done. If the husband wants to play golf at weekends, then he needs to be able to do that. As long as the interests don't get in the way of the relationship, both parties to a marriage should give way a little and encourage their partner to do things that they always wanted to.

So how do you find out your partner's dreams?

During conversations of an intimate kind, you can go back to the time when you first met and bring up subjects that were part of your everyday life. "I remember I used to think I would become a ballroom dancer." may be responded to by "Then why not take up classes? You still have the interest." If your partner doesn't know what your wishes are, then it's likely that those wishes will get swept under the carpet. You can't blame your partner because you never mentioned them, but somehow you do blame him because you feel that you have been stopped from doing something that you really want to do.

What about your partner? How about mentioning the fact that he used to enjoy golf? You may spark off a conversation that he really benefits from. And it's not just golf. Girls like to get together for girly nights and boys like the same thing. Often people put off all of the things that make them independent just because they are married. Put the excitement back into your life and try being honest about your feelings and the things that you want to do. Nothing happens to improve the situation without input from both of you.

I remember friends that used to drive me nuts. She let him take control of everything. If they went anywhere, he drove. If they bought anything, he had to approve of it. If she went out, he took her. They didn't have any independence whatsoever as a couple. Then, in her menopause years, she suddenly realized there was no sparkle left in the relationship because she always knew that he got the last say in everything. She wanted to rebel and frankly, no one could have blamed her, but she had put up with this kind of behavior for so long that she didn't know how to rebel. In fact, no one was more shocked than her husband to learn how unhappy she was and to learn that it was also his fault that she was unhappy. On their 30th wedding anniversary, he started to put that right and bought her a car all of her own.

Men need to remember that Miss Independent that they married may now feel tied to a kitchen sink by motherhood. Women who are accustomed to adult conversation may resent being at home all day with kids and still want that adult conversation. Therefore, there need to be breaks from the monotony of marriage to keep the sparkle alive. A marriage isn't made up of one strong person and his/her counterpart. It is made of two people and that needs to be remembered at all times. If you feel that either you or your partner isn't the same independent person that they used to be, then it's time to recognize that individuality and celebrate it. If he loved golf when he was younger, how about buying him clubs? If she loved tennis when she was younger, how about membership of the local tennis club? It's not just about sports. It's about having "me" time and if you can treat each other to that "me" time when your partner can indulge in pleasurable pursuits, then it helps the marriage no end.

Responsibilities that you find within a marriage can kill all of those dreams. Buy an easel and get out the oil paints. Do the things you always wanted to. Your husband/wife married you because of who YOU are – rather than what responsibility makes you into. When independence in re-introduced into the picture, happy people are able to emerge from the shadows and gain respect for each other. That's vital to a good marriage and is something that you need to bear in mind. Someone asked me once "isn't it selfish that I should want to go on vacation alone?" and my answer was that it wasn't at all selfish. She loved the beach. He hated it and would much prefer to go around museums. She had been dragged around museums for the last ten years of her life and it wasn't much pleasure for him having a reluctant wife with him. They started to take separate vacations and found the day that they got back together again gave them a fresh start every time with both of them happier for it. It's not fair to drag your partner into your dreams or for them to drag you into theirs, but if you can find a middle path, this is the one that will make both of you happy.

The best way to find out what your partner is interested in is to actually ask, though if a wife has been compliant to your wishes for a long time, it may take more than that. You need to remember the time when you first met and try to think of things that appeared to interest your partner when he/she was single. Get into conversations about it and find out what kind of things your partner would enjoy doing. Kelly was quite surprised when her husband showed that he was interested in Thai Chi, as he had never expressed an interest in the past. However, he was then able to share all of the photos from his mom's album of the things that he collected when he was a kid that were all martial arts related and she began to know another side of her husband that she had never seen before. She, on the other hand, had always wanted to try archery. At the county fair, she had always had a go, so he had a clue that she enjoyed it. When she joined the club, their different interests fit in well with each other and they were both able to follow their passion without letting this get in the way of them being a couple.

The problem that a lot of married people make is that they are too easily pulled into the routine of their partner, rather than making waves. When interests are discussed, you also need to respect your partner and understand that your partner may also have interests that need catering for. Thus, when you buy your Thai Chi outfit, you need to make sure there's enough left in the bank to buy her those classes that she wants.

There are so many resentments caused by one partner having an outside interest and the other being pulled into it. That interest can range from sports to having a motor home. It could be stamp collecting – or it could be collecting memorabilia. If you don't respect your partner's interests equally, then you are setting yourself up for a disappointed partner. No married person should simply go along with their partner's interests because they feel they have to. In fact, retaining your independence is paramount. Thus, when you know that you want to be doing something and are not sure how to introduce that to the dynamics of the relationship, the best way is openness. Be open about your interests. Tell your partner that you do not expect him/her to be interested in those things but that you would like to continue to have your interests. Watch how he/she reacts. If your partner needs extra reassurance that this independence is not taking you away from him/her, then make sure that you give that reassurance. Tell your partner that at the end of the day, having your own interests will make you a more complete and happy person and that he/she will benefit from it because a happier person is easier to live with!

Takeaways from this chapter:

You could be married for more than 40 years. Therefore, you need to be yourself and, when your needs are met, you are likely to be a happier and more fulfilled person. Thus, think of yourself as fulfilled rather than thinking of yourself as selfish if you want to follow your heart and take up interests that are not on your partner's agenda. It's important that you have good roots to your relationship but that doesn't mean that one of you should stagnate to placate the other.

1. Talk about interests and let your partner know who you are
2. Take up interests and enjoy talking to your partner about his/her interests
3. Be an individual and don't just fall into "liking" the same things. It may happen, but let it happen because you want to learn rather than feel obliged to.
4. Laugh about all of your childhood ambitions together

5. Make a bucket list of things you want to achieve in your life and aim for them together. Even if they are not the same, don't dismiss them because these are wishes that people make about the things they want to achieve in life.
6. Help your partner to achieve his/her dreams

Forty years may seem a long time, but that's not the longest marriage on record. The record goes to a couple who were married for 90 years and 123 days. This was a couple that lived in the United Kingdom. Karam Chand was interviewed about his long marriage and the advice that he gave was wise:

"The key to a happy marriage is getting along together and being family focused."

That's a very simple key to happiness, although if you add the ingredient of respecting each other's interests, you add a new dimension to the marriage and make it a place where two people can cohabit happily giving mutual respect to each other's hopes and dreams. In the case of Karam Chand and his wife, his family was the biggest joy to him and produced eight children and twenty seven grandchildren. One thing I did notice in the interview was the emphasis on good food, which seemed to be a passion to Mrs. Chand. They also traveled a lot together and shared lifestyles living in different continents. You may not be married for as long as this couple, but there is no reason why your marriage should not be every bit as happy as theirs was. Give your partner room to breathe, to embrace his/her interests and you can enjoy a very long and happy relationship.

Chapter 7: The Compliments

"When someone who loves and cares about me compliments me, I feel more glamorous than when the flashbulbs are going off on the red carpet."

~ Gabrielle Union

When you live a very mundane life where you are getting up and going to work every day, sometimes one of the things that slips into the background are compliments. Men forget to tell their women how nice they look or how proud they are of them because there never seems to be the right time. Make time. It will make the world of difference. It isn't just about bolstering your partner's self-confidence levels. It's about something much deeper than that. When your partner admires you for something you are capable of doing, it makes you feel good inside and reinforces why you are with that partner in the first place.

However – beware

If you are too generous with your compliments, these come out as insincere and meaningless. The timing of compliments is essential. You man has his friends over for the game. How about serving up something really nice and letting them know that you love your husband by being extra affectionate. If you compliment him/her in front of their friends that really does do a whole lot for their egos. It reinforces your love for them and it also reinforces why they love you. When I say about people being over-generous with their compliments, I mean it. A man who calls everybody "darling" won't get much extra from his wife by using this compliment because she knows he uses it too much anyway. It comes over as false flattery. You need to be sincere.

Tackling insecurities

There are various stages that people go through in their lives that cause insecurity. When a woman's hair starts to go gray, she may feel old and wrinkled. It's nice when her husband tells her that she will never be old and wrinkled to him. Similarly, a man with a slightly podgy waistline may feel like he is getting old, but it doesn't hurt to reassure him that you love him, even though there's more of him now than there used to be. Think about it logically. When a child stands for the first time, that child is very unsure. When teens go through puberty, they are very unsure of themselves as well. There's no rule that says that this uncertainty will stop just because you are an adult. In fact, it's a truth that uncertainty can follow you all of your life.

Thus, the compliments that you give help to firm up your partner's belief in him/herself and that's going to add to the happiness factor. Women lose confidence during stages such as childbirth, being a parent, going through menopause etc. but they may also lose it due to all kinds of other things. Rejection in the workplace, workplace problems, family problems and things like this will always touch the way that your wife feels in her life. Your compliments boost her self-esteem and make her feel better and that's needed in a good marriage. For a man, he may doubt his masculinity as his waist gets larger. He may not like the fact that his hair is receding or that it's going gray. No one likes all the extra lines on their face. Thus, when she compliments him, it makes him feel better about himself as well.

If you are going to be in a relationship for the long haul, expect changes because these happen because of life. If you are ready for those changes and remember that your partner is experiencing them too, you can stop any damage that these may do just by remembering that your partner needs to know he/she is vital to you. It is easy to get into a rut in life and to let the mundane take over. However, that bunch of wild flowers you stopped to pick for her may make all the difference to her day. The fact that you didn't just flex a plastic card to get her flowers counts as one of the biggest compliments you can give her. That shows love and respect for her. Similarly, when she compliments him by having the table set for a candlelit dinner and has sent the kids packing to their grandparents for the night - that shows him that he's important and that she wants to celebrate the marriage with HIM and no one else.

Compliments are the little things that you do for each other out of respect. When you hold the door open for her, when she reaches out to take his coat – these are all compliments of the most intimate type that show care and devotion and these are what make marriages a great place to be. Compliments are a powerful demonstration of care. They are what is missing from the average day. They are missing from relationships where people take each other for granted, but when you reintroduce them into the relationship, they bring back that sparkle of mutual respect that makes each partner remember why they fell in love with their partner in the first place. It's very much a two-way thing and if you start introducing positive reinforcement to your partner, it won't be long until they return the compliment. Then, life gets to be fun together, knowing that you have some attribute that your partner approves of and loves.

Eloise always used to tell everyone she was a bad cook. However, her cooking improved over the course of her marriage and this was intentional. She wanted to be a good wife. She wanted to be able to provide really good food for her family and had lived with the reputation of being a bad cook for most of her life. It surprised her husband when she started to make the most delicious food, and he complimented her on it. The other thing that she found very endearing was that he stood up for her when family members criticized her cooking. "He was actually telling them that they were out of touch and that I was one of the best cooks going!" She couldn't believe how much this bolstered her confidence. When there is teasing going on, sometimes, it's taken seriously and people do what they can to improve their skills. If your partner does this, do compliment him/her because it makes it all worthwhile.

During the course of a marriage, a husband or wife may at some time try to become more efficient at something because they feel that they want to evolve as a person and gain confidence. For example, Henry wasn't much good at fixing things around the house, but when he applied himself, he was able to do a fairly good job. His wife complimented him and what happened as a result of those compliments was that he learned more because the compliments gave him a new enthusiasm that he had not felt before.

Whatever it is that your partner does that is compliment worthy is worth mentioning because without anyone actually noticing all those good things, chances are that the good behavior – in whatever form – will stop because your partner will feel that there's not much point in improving if no one ever notices. If you have been working on your relationship and your partner has made an extra effort to pull all the stops out to please you, celebrate it. Make them feel special. That's what makes your partner feel that he/she is on the right track and is likely to bring forward all kinds of good things within the marriage. Jacquie wanted wallpaper in her living room, but knew that her husband had no idea how to put it up. She encouraged him and said that they would be okay if they did it together and worked out all of the intricacies between them. This gave him the enthusiasm to try and, between them, they made a pretty good job of it. If you show confidence in your partner and when things get difficult, offer a little help, you will be surprised at what they can do. Often it's the lack of enthusiasm and support and indeed the criticism of their character that stops them in their tracks. A compliment and a little support go a very long way and if you want to gain compliments, instead of fishing for them, try giving a few yourself because they really do make your partner feel good and people who feel good are liable to be more generous with their compliments.

Takeaways from this chapter

Different people have different levels of security. The woman who was teased in her youth for being overweight may actually have grown up with a complex about how she looks. If a man takes the time to compliment her when she has truly made an effort, he is likely to give her more confidence and make her happier. Similarly, men may feel they don't match up to others. In society today, the media dictates what we should expect from a man and from a woman. We see the role models on TV and suddenly people feel that they don't match up to the expectations others have of them. Ask yourself how many women would look great on the cover of Cosmopolitan or how many men would be suitable to feature on the front pages of a magazine aimed at women. The answer is that only small percentages meet up with that kind of expectation.

Compliments are an affirmation. They can positively lift someone from a situation of ill ease and make them feel on top of the world. James was born short. As he got older, he began to see people around him and felt he didn't measure up. His wife, Judith, thought differently. When she became aware of his insecurity, she was the first to tell him that the size of a man didn't mean much at all and was merely a physical attribute. What mattered to her was the sentiment of the man and she expressed how happy she was married to him. Those compliments should always be at the right time and should be sincere. Instead of looking at the weaknesses of your partner, look at their strengths and celebrate them, because this is when you find out your own strengths and weaknesses.

Being aware of the ability of your partner is a wonderful addition to your relationship. For example, the woman whose husband stopped to pick her flowers knew that he was thoughtful and kind but that instead of using his credit card, he had actually taken the time to stop his car and pick the flowers, knowing her preference. The man whose wife prepared him a supper that was very similar to one they had on honeymoon is reminded about how thoughtful his wife is and should never avoid expressing approval because this adds a wealth to a relationship that can overcome the hurdles that life poses.

Affirmations are something taught by life coaches all over the world. If you can find that kind of positivity in your relationship, it helps you to get through hard times because the positive vibes between you and your partner are always enhanced by appreciation of each other. Compliments help you to demonstrate this positivity. The next time that someone compliments you, take a mental note of how it made you feel. That's why compliments are so positive. They affirm the importance of someone and help to make them feel great. They also help you to see clearly the good things about your partner and your relationship, rather than dwelling on the negative aspects. Negativity breeds negativity and positivity charges a relationship with a new kind of energy. This energy helps you to gain confidence, and your partner needs that kind of confidence too. Thus, don't be afraid of letting your partner know their strengths, rather than dwelling on their weaknesses.

Chapter 8: Dealing with Mistakes and Shame

"If we can share our story with someone who responds with empathy and understanding, shame can't survive."

Brene Brown

If you have ever been in a long-term relationship, you will know that things happen that may cause distance between you and your spouse. For example, the alcoholic who decides to sneak a drink may keep that kind of information from his/her spouse because of shame. The woman who loses her job when she knows that the mortgage needs paying and her husband is depending upon her to bring in a set amount a month may feel shame. Shame is the destroyer of relationships but it doesn't have to be. If you want to get your relationship back on track after a shameful episode of some kind, you have to ask yourself these questions:

- Can I get beyond this and prove myself to my partner?

- Do I trust my partner enough to be honest?

- Do I trust myself sufficiently to get past this?

- Can I depend upon my partner to help me get past this?

If you find yourself in the unfortunate situation of something going wrong, you need to work out a way beyond it and you also need to trust your partner sufficiently to ask for their help. This is vital to getting beyond the problem. You can't hide it. There is nowhere to hide within a marriage. If you try to, you are showing lack of trust for your partner and probably don't deserve to be in a good relationship. You have to learn that trust is part and parcel of what happens when you get into a long-term relationship or marriage.

Unfortunately, the mistrust is something that can creep into a relationship and when it does, you are in trouble. You promise that you will remember to do something and then don't remember. You promise to make a phone call and then forget to make it and your partner asks you if you did what you were supposed to and in an attempt to cover up your mistake, you tell a lie. If you have ever done this, you need to learn how to stop doing it in the future. Every time that you introduce doubt into your relationship, it causes deeper damage than you may be aware of. This is only a small incident, you may say, but if it's only a small incident, why did you find it necessary to lie about it? Why couldn't you just admit that you forgot? This is where people who live together often go wrong.

So how do you get over shame or blame?

The best way forward when you have done something wrong is to be totally upfront about it and admit it. "Oh goodness me, I forgot. I am so sorry." It may seem hard to say at first, but it puts an end to it all. You don't have to feel the shame anymore because your partner will know what the score is and you don't have to feel shame because you lied. It sounds like common sense but in many instances, one small lie leads to a series of lies. If you are found out for a lie, your partner is put on some kind of alert. "What else is he/she lying about?" and lack of trust in a relationship will really kill it stone dead. If you have done something wrong, regardless of the gravity of the situation, choose a time to sit down and level with your partner about it.

"I lost my job. I don't have any severance pay so I am not sure how we can pay the mortgage this month."

What you are doing in this instance is opening up what you see as a can of worms, but you have to understand that if your partner knows what the situation is, there are now two people working on the problem and it's easier for them, as a couple, to come up with solutions. Perhaps the partner who is working can adjust their hours to reap a little more pay. Perhaps the family can help while you look for another job. If you are honest about it and don't use shame as an excuse to distance yourself from your partner, things work out much more quickly than if you try to keep it all to yourself.

"I forgot to pick up the dry cleaning today. I am so sorry. I had too much on my mind."

This alerts your partner to the fact that you are stressed. It alerts your partner to the fact that you have something on your mind and it gives your partner the opportunity to help take a little of the weight from you. Mistakes are going to happen at some stage during your marriage. It's a pretty obvious thing to accept although those who use subterfuge to hide shame are really putting their relationship at risk. It's never worth being so ashamed of yourself that you cannot discuss it with your partner. Tell your partner of your shame. Let your partner see that you truly are sorry for any inconvenience and if you find it hard to approach your partner, try to talk about it when you and your partner have sufficient time on your own to discuss what it is that is bothering you.

Emily was married to a man who told her lies. She fell head over heels in love with the guy and every time he told lies, she knew they were lies, but she made excuses for him. Even her friends would tell her that she needed to confront him but she refused to. In the end, the guy was so used to telling her lies that slipping into a love affair with someone else, Emily had made it very easy for him to have all the time he needed to see his mistress. He explained the situation in this way:

"I was a drinker. I was ashamed of telling Emily and I didn't want her to have to worry about it. She gave me too loose a reign and I met others who had the same problem. Ingrid was one of those people. She understood my drinking problem because she had one as well and we drifted into a relationship. In retrospect, I wish I had been open with Emily. It cost me my marriage and I deserved everything that I got. The trouble is that sometimes wives or partners in general see you with rose colored spectacles and put you onto a pedestal that you are bound to fall off."

He is right to a certain degree that partners who believe their spouse to be beyond reproach often do hold them to high standards and it is their high level of expectation that makes it very difficult for the erring partner to actually talk about problems that may be occurring. "It would have broken Emily's heart to tell her that I was an alcoholic," he explained, "although I now know that having gotten over the initial shock, Emily would have done anything to help me. I was shortsighted in not telling her."

In a relationship, you need two-way communication. We keep saying this, but when you have done something wrong – instead of letting this alienate you from the one you love, talk about it. It is vital that you are able to share and that means sharing everything – good and bad. When you made those vows at the altar, they included "better and worse" and there is barely a person on earth who goes through a lifetime without making some kind of mistake. Therefore, being able to admit your mistake is the best way forward. You show remorse. You convince your partner that you are sorry and if you need to enlist your partner's help to get over a bad situation, your partner will probably be only too happy to help. That's far better than keeping secrets from someone that you are supposed to love and trust.

There are times when I look back on the marriages of people who have passed through my office with marital problems that I realize what a big problem this is and indeed that it merits a chapter. Instead of disappointing your partner with lies, make a point that you will always be truthful. Make a point that if you have problems, you will not hide them because doing so shows a decided lack of trust in your partner and although you may see that you are doing this for all the right reasons or to protect your partner from hurt, long term you are making things worse and that's not going to help your relationship. Your partner is stronger than you give him/her credit for and can help you through these problems if you let that happen instead of hiding the things that you are ashamed of or sorry for.

Takeaways from this chapter:

In this chapter, we dealt with shame. If you are going to spend a whole lifetime with someone, you are going to have to deal with shame at some stage in your relationship. It may not even be between you and your spouse. It may be that your children are ashamed of not following parental advice. However, be bigger than the shame by following the rules that are shown here:

1. Accept that people make mistakes and comfort your spouse.

2. Help your spouse to overcome his/her difficulties if you can.
3. Never add to the shame by making your spouse feel even worse about what they have done wrong. It helps no one and is destructive to the marriage.
4. Try not to hide secrets from your partner unless of course they are nice surprises.
5. Above all, be honest about your own mistakes.
6. Learn together about how to overcome those hurdles that present themselves.

By following these rules, you can get beyond shame and put your relationship back onto an equal footing. If you carry that shame with you and constantly remind your partner of his/her shortcomings, you are readying yourself for the divorce courts. The next chapter deals with the kind of lies that will inevitably lead to divorce. Be aware of them and if you have done something wrong, you'll want to ask yourself how valuable your marriage is, as this will tell you how to deal with them. If you believe that your partner cannot help you, but that you need specialist help – such as in the case of having a drinking problem – you still need to explain to your partner that you acknowledge your problem. You can then look into ways to seek professional help together.

Acceptance of your partner, regardless of his/her faults, is all part and parcel of the normal course of events in marriage. You cannot be perfect. There is no such thing as a perfect person. Thus, you need to acknowledge your faults and share them, so that, as a couple, you can overcome the problems together.

Chapter 9 : Lies that lead to Divorce

"I'm not upset that you lied to me. I am upset that from now on, I can't believe you."

~ Friedrich Nietzsche

There is a lot of relevance to the quotation I chose to begin this chapter. The trouble is that when you lie, you start to begin mistrust. Trust is essential in a relationship. If the trust is gone, it is very hard to rebuild it. It can be done. There are couples who are able to get beyond trust issues and sustain their relationships, but it makes it very hard. In everyday life, you tend not to trust people who lie to you. It is natural that you should feel this way. From childhood, you learn all about the relevance of lies from your parents. People who tell lies are bad people. This follows you into adulthood and the first thing that people think about when they are told a lie is that they cannot trust that person to tell them the truth. That, in a marriage, is catastrophic.

In this chapter, we deal with the kind of lies that people tell which may threaten a relationship, especially a relationship as close as marriage. When you first get married, you make vows to each other that include being faithful and supportive of your spouse. You may not have made the promise to be faithful. That rather depends upon the wording of the ceremony. However, it goes without saying that you are expected to be true to the person you choose to marry. You may be surprised at some of the lies that can lead to the divorce courts but it is necessary to show you what these are so that you recognize them and can stem this kind of behavior before your marriage leads to a dead end.

Seeing marriage as a contract – Not only is this insulting to your partner, but it also shows lack of respect. This may be used as the kind of gesture that is cruel. Marriage isn't a contract. Yes, you go through legal formalities, but the end result is that two people have chosen to live together and to exchange vows that go much deeper than any legal contract ever could. The sentiment between the two parties should always mean more than a piece of paper. If you ever feel tempted to remind your loved one that you are in a contractual situation with him/her, think twice. This is contemptable and is not an acceptable response even if you feel like you are in a bad situation. It belittles love. It makes your partner feel like the union means no more than purchasing a house or a car. It makes your partner into a commodity. Do not be tempted into using this lie. If you felt enough to marry your partner, you obviously saw the relationship as more than a contract and if you are seeing marriage in that way, then you have a lot of work to do to make up for your lack of compassion.

I am not married to my in-laws – One source of anger between a man and wife comes from the extended family that he takes on as his own or that she takes on once the marriage vows are made. The relationship between your spouse and his family doesn't end just because you are married. If you find that the family is making demands that are unreasonable, you need to approach the subject in a very subtle way, remembering that these are people who formed part of your partner's life long before you came on the scene. They will still be his relatives long after you have parted. You may not appreciate the way that your in-laws act toward you. However, you do need to learn to stand your ground, bearing in mind that you should do nothing to harm the relationship between family and your spouse.

In the case of Jacqueline and Steve, Jacqueline found that constant criticism from her mother in law was getting on her nerves. She insisted that her husband choose between his mother and her. Wishing to keep the peace, Steve agreed that he would have less contact with his mother. Over the next couple of years, the resentment between Jacqueline and her husband built up to a crescendo. Jacqueline expected Steve to choose her over his mother and when his mother died, he could never forgive her for making him make that choice. They ultimately divorced. Your in-laws are your in-laws and no amount of wishful thinking can change that. If you can learn to tolerate their interaction with your family, that's the best way to go forward, knowing that as soon as they leave, you can live your family life in any manner you choose.

I can't change who I am – This is one of the biggest cop-outs. What you are really saying is that if your spouse doesn't like the situation you are creating, tough luck. It shows that you have absolutely no intention of compromising and the problem with an attitude such as this is that you alienate loved ones by being so obstinate. Most people can change to fit into a relationship. If you cannot, you should not have been married in the first place.

It didn't mean anything – This is the excuse that is often used after unfaithfulness. It belittles making love and trivializes it. If that didn't mean anything, why did it happen? The problem with this excuse is that it shows as transparent that your wedding vows didn't mean anything either. When you are unfaithful to your spouse, you break any trust there may be between you and no excuses – let alone weak ones – will make that infidelity go away.

It's not you, it's me – This is the way that people justify negative feelings toward a spouse. They try to make the blow gentler by blaming themselves, although in reality, they have already decided that the relationship isn't working for them. The spouse then tries to help and makes the situation even less acceptable. If you hear these words, ask for an explanation. It may be a passing problem that you can work around or it may mean that as far as your partner is concerned, the relationship is already over. By asking for an explanation, you are able to discern whether the phrase was used as a signing off of the relationship or whether this is a temporary situation.

There are of course many more lies that may land you in trouble, but the rule of thumb is that you think before you speak or act if you want to keep the intimacy that it may have taken years to create between you. Even small lies can start to erode the intimacy and every element of doubt that you introduce into the relationship will have a negative ripple.

Conversely, in the next chapter, we are going to deal with what makes love grow because it's no good just looking at the negative side of situations. You also need to be able to understand the structure of a relationship and how that relationship is able to flourish. Little additions to your normal activities and little gestures on a positive note can make the world of difference.

Janine heard the words "It's not you, it's me" when she was troubled by her husband's sudden interest with being away from the home. She was about to have a baby and expected her husband to be more supportive rather than less supportive. In their case, she cared enough to find out why this was happening. Apparently, when his mother had given birth to him, his father had left her. With all of the feelings of insecurity he felt about the new baby, he was afraid that these feelings were leading to wanting to escape. However, he loved his wife so much that he thought if he was away from home more, he had more time to work out in his mind what was happening to him. He had no intention of leaving but his background told him that some men just can't face becoming fathers. The insecurity he was feeling was unfamiliar to him. However, as soon as Janine knew what it was all about, she made a point of involving him in every aspect and he became a very proud father. His reticence was simply feeling out of control of the situation and not knowing if he had what it takes to be a good father.

Takeaways from this chapter:

A lie is always a lie no matter how much you attempt to make it trivial. A relationship is built up of mutual trust. Trust is something that can be destroyed by lies and little ones add up into big ones. If you want your relationship to survive and to thrive, you need to understand that truth is part of the picture. If your wife asks for your honest opinion about the dress she has bought, that doesn't mean to say you should insult her if you don't like it. You can be honest without hurting her feelings by telling her that you prefer another dress that she wears. Believe it or not, when she is tuned into you, she will know the difference and will thank you for being kind. You need to consider the following points when you consider lies:

1. What the lie hides
2. Whether the lie is harmful or meant in jest
3. If the lie is something you cannot talk about with your partner, then your relationship may be in trouble.

4. If your partner lies to you, you need to understand why. Talk about it to establish the reasons.
5. If the reason for a lie is self-doubt, you may be able to move forward in your relationship by helping your loved one through a difficult situation.
6. If the reason for the lie is plain deception, then it's time to re-evaluate whether the relationship is worth continuing.

When trust is broken, any continued lies will completely erode that trust and when there is no trust left, you don't have a relationship upon which you can build any more. Think of mutual trust as being that element that forms the roots of a relationship. If the roots are bad, the relationship cannot grow and flourish. If you find that your partner lacks confidence, help him/her to gain that confidence. For example, Kelly told her husband that she had an interest in football. After years of putting up with missing out on her favorite TV shows, she finally admitted that she really didn't enjoy sports. They were able to mend the situation by buying her a TV so that they could both enjoy themselves equally. Had Jerry known earlier, he would have helped her out of the situation sooner. Lies don't really help anyone – even small ones. Now that they understand each other better, their marriage is a lot happier. They joke about the football whenever Jerry thinks that his wife is telling white lies trying to please others. He knows it's her nature to be kind and to lack consideration for herself. Now, with his jokes, he is able to remind her that her thoughts are just as important as his and that she has a right to her own opinion. Through his love, she has managed to gain confidence and become happier.

Whenever a lie happens, or whenever a doubt is aired, talk about it because it can bring you closer rather than placing a wedge between you. Relationships are complex and consist of negative and positive emotions. Learn to understand them both as you may find that the lie was told because of fear of hurting your feelings. Show your loved one that your feelings are stronger than he/she supposed and embrace the truth together. If the truth is too hard to swallow and has already eroded the roots of the relationship, then you can do no more than close the final page of the book.

Chapter 10 : What Makes Love Grow

"You know you're in love when you can't fall asleep because reality is finally better than your dreams."

Dr. Seuss

You may have ideas that romance and romantic feelings are what make love grow but there's much more to it than that. Sometimes you can look across the room at your partner and feel a certain pride at the fact that your partner chose you out of all of the possibilities in the world. There are magical things that make love grow, but there are ordinary things as well. You may look up from your breakfast bowl and see that all too familiar smile on your partner's face. You may wake up in the morning and see your partner sleeping and recapture that amazing feeling that this is the love of your life. Expect that to be intermingled with times when you look at your partner and wonder what made you choose him/her for a lifetime partner. It's all part of the rich tapestry of life. If you were in love 24 hours a day, life would be difficult because there are times when you need a much more controlled attitude that isn't tinged by thoughts of love. For example, the practical things that will happen during the course of a marriage will quickly bring you down to Earth. So people ask me what makes love grow and is grown love any better than that feeling you get when you fall in love?

In fact, mature love is better than the first pangs of passion because it's surer. There are no disappointments and you know exactly where you stand with that person you have chosen. There are times when you know how much that love has matured. For example, you will surprise yourself by being able to deal with illness or difficulties that you may not have been able to deal with when you were younger. Why? Because love enables you to be there at the right time and say all of the right things to help the situation to pass.

When Colin got cancer, his wife questions "Why him?" and going through all the process of treatment with him, found strength in the love that they felt for one another. She was able to tell him off when she thought that he was being overly dramatic. He was able to let her know when he thought that she should be more sympathetic. However, when he went in for an operation, she stayed at the hospital and because the guest beds were so uncomfortable, slept on a mattress on the floor. As he looked toward her, he knew that it was only a mature love that would go to those lengths to give him the support that he needed. He was happy that she was there and she was happy to be there. Mature love knows no real boundaries and it isn't half as afraid as new love is. The passion is different too but that's not through lack of trying. Many people, as they get older, find they are limited in what they can do to show passion, but passion comes in many different guises and isn't confined to what sexual positions you can muster. It happens when you pass each other and touch skin. It happens when you look into your partner's eyes and don't have to say anything because the words are understood.

The love that you have grows but in a mature way and it is by going through all of the different events that you may expect in a lifetime that the roots get firmly entrenched, so that both parties have confidence that their partner will never let them down. That's true love and it is lasting love and although some may see this kind of love as lacking in passion, what it makes up for in emotional security makes it worth it.

Way back in the '60s, there was a cartoonist who put all of this mundanity into perspective by creating the "Love is ..." cartoons, which depicted ordinary everyday situations in which people prove their growing love for one another. These were created by a New Zealander by the name of Kim Casali. What she did was extremely clever because this was at a time when the youth of the day were looking for more out of love than a semi-detached house and a mortgage. One could almost describe this era as being the "love and peace" era, but her cartoons took normal everyday situations and explained what love actually was. For example, a picture of two people in cartoon format show a man bringing in a tray with a cup of tea for his wife and the caption is "Love is ... When nothing is too much trouble."

It may be a good idea to have a look at some of these because there will be situations within your lives which will be shown on the cartoons. Love matures and grows and the courtesies that you show to one another all add to the scope of that love. "Love is... Finding time for each other" is depicted by the couple being seated on the hands of a clock. There is a lot of common sense in many of the cartoons and, over the years, people have expanded upon the message using these cartoons for greetings cards and for notes sent from one spouse to another.

You don't have to do anything special for that love to grow. Learning to trust your partner at all times and letting your partner have sufficient confidence in you to trust you helps over the years. Surprise your partner occasionally by remembering who you both used to be. A candle lit dinner may not be your thing and it's not a standard prerequisite for reaffirming your love. If you have something special that means the same to the two of you – whether that's a picnic by the river or carving your names on a tree – then these are the things that mean the earth to both of you and that help keep the roots of your love firmly planted. One couple we talked to planted a tree at the birth of each of their children and now that the children have left the nest, the trees remain, big and strong as a reminder of the passage of time. All of these things help love to grow and mature and whatever floats your boat, as a couple is what will make that love stronger and more dependable. Another couple had a passion for garage sales and had built a wonderful home filled with all of the treasures that they had found together. That time spent together meant that they were sharing a common bond that both of them were interested in and which gave them something to talk about.

I remember one couple saying that they could not imagine their parents feeling that way for one another, but when I asked them to be more observant, they actually found the clues that they had missed all of those years of growing up. Her parents had a signal system between them and although they never appeared to be outwardly loving, the growth of their love was evident in the secret language that they used between each other to share amusing moments. His parents, on the other hand, were able to show their love for each other through their work together on the farm. You will find that the things that make love grow are not the things that you buy or that you shower your loved one with. They grow from the words that you say and even the unspoken words that you both know just by looking at each other. They also grow from experiences that you share.

A mature love is a very precious thing that gives you confidence that your partner will always be there for you. It lasts a lifetime and is worth every bit of effort put into the relationship. Try leaving him a rose on his pillow. You may be surprised to note that it isn't just women who like the romantic gestures. Some men may be happy to sport the pullover that she made for him, while others are just as happy sharing an umbrella on a wet and windy day. Love grows from small gestures and when you have a mature love, you know never to take it for granted, though can bask in its security.

Takeaways from this chapter:

It isn't always the obvious things that help love to grow. You don't have to shower your partner with gifts and you certainly don't have to do things that are portrayed by the media as being romantic. A growing love contains the following elements:

1. Shared experiences and emotions
2. Trust in each other and mutual respect
3. Never harboring resentments
4. Being able to avoid taking each other for granted
5. Being in synch with the emotions of your loved one
6. Knowing the boundaries and respecting them

All of the elements of love depend upon honesty, trust and mutual respect. If you try to force love, you need to look inwardly to see why you are so insecure. True love grows through experience, rather than being something that you can force. The more you try to force love, the less likely it is to be able to be free to grow. Alice and Jim had five children. They were never rich, but they considered themselves to be very rich in that the security they found in each other's company was sufficient to make their lives happier. As their children grew and left home, the love within the family grew to encompass all of the grandchildren. It was a completely secure love, borne of hard work together and knowing each other's strengths and weaknesses. When asked about the things that they would change about their partners, they joked because neither could imagine trading in their partner for anyone else. "I may change her obstinacy," joked Jim but Alice was very quick to retort. "If you did that, you would have no one to set you right when you make mistakes!" She was probably right and so was he. They had found that their love had grown and matured to such an extent that they were comfortable in making criticisms of each other in a joking way. Their love accepted both the good and the bad and didn't distinguish between the two.

Remember:

1. Love accepts what is, rather than trying to change it
2. Love supports times that are bad and one person's strengths make up for another's weaknesses.
3. Love doesn't walk away when things become difficult
4. Love is there when there is little else left

The growth of love depends upon each couple showing each other a level of trust and companionship. Love and trust go hand in hand, just as mutual respect becomes a part of the picture. When you are able to accept your partner's bad points as well as his/her good ones, you know that the footing of your relationship is solid and that love is maturing. That's very important. When you are a young bride or groom, you don't even imagine the kind of things that age will throw at you, though a love that is secure will be able to deal with those elements of life that are unpredictable and help you through them.

I have included this chapter because many couples that come for advice cannot see beyond the moment that they are in. They see problematic marriages and are not sure that these can survive the different storms of life. However, you also need to remember that mothers and fathers have the same doubts about their abilities to bring up kids. It's a natural progression. It just happens and when it does, you will know that your love is something that has matured and grown with you.

Chapter 11: Knowing What Intimacy is All About

"It is an absolute human certainty that no one can know his own beauty or perceive a sense of his own worth until it has been reflected back to him in the mirror of another loving, caring human being."

~ John Joseph Powell

There are many people who misunderstand what intimacy is. They may think it only relates to sexual activity, but it happens long before sexual relations begin. Intimacy is that feeling of being inside a bubble with someone else. You are on the same page, in the same frame of mind and share a moment that no one else is aware of. When you meet that lover for the first time and know you are going to become lovers that feeling inside you is the seed of intimacy. When you start to talk and find that your chemistry is turned on by this conversation, that's what intimacy is. When you can look across a room and signal your intentions with your eyes without saying a word, that's a kind of intimacy too.

Talking to people who have been married for years, you may get the old jokes about intimacy becoming a cup of cocoa and a hot water bottle, but that's got very little to do with intimacy at all. That's just sexual innuendo. The joke is that she always has a headache or that he snores and takes away the idea of romance, but neither of these are really anything to do with intimacy.

If you look up the meaning of the word, you may be surprised. "An affinity, a close rapport, close relationship" are words that describe intimacy, although I like the association with the word "affinity" because it kind of means being wrapped around something to such an extent that it begins to be part of who you are. Imagine then if you both like that cocoa in bed, you can have a great intimate moment sitting in bed and indulging in it, because that's the affinity between you. It's a joining between two people and it really doesn't have to be sexual at all. That closeness or affinity is almost like two human beings being knotted together in a figure of eight where you can't see where one person begins or ends. It's a closeness like no other.

Somewhere along the line, there have to be events within your relationship that only you and your partner understand and can smile about. These can be sexual but they don't have to be. You need to remember them and reintroduce those looks that tell your partner you really are wrapped up in what message he is sending you, or look out for signs that your partner is wrapped up in you. It may show in the wink of an eye. It may simply be something you both feel at the same time. You are so close to that particular person that your thoughts intertwine and belong to each other.

If you think about the practicalities of marriage, a lot of time is spent on doing things that are necessary and sometimes, that leaves very little time for doing things that give you pleasure. However, on a quiet evening when you have time to spend together, even if that is only for a short time, how about going over the old photographs and the old memories? It works wonders and it brings back to life all of the things that you have shared in the past and makes them relevant to the moment.

I could actually sit at a dinner party and signal to my partner many different things that other people would not understand or even notice. When you are that close to another human being you can do that. A small twinkle in the eye may signal something to your partner that they remember from the past. Try it and see where it leads. You need to keep intimate channels open between you. You may even enjoy a truth or dare game together that brings back all of these intimate memories. Base it on your relationship and make the rule that all questions must refer to the marriage.

Do you remember that quiz show on TV where they question one partner about the other and have to try and come up with the right answers? It's actually surprising but many couples don't know each other as well as they think they do, and playing games such as this with the sole purpose of getting closer is always going to be a good thing. I always thought that my partner preferred me in blue until we played this game when in fact it was my partner's least favorite color on me. When I learned my partner's preference, I could avoid blue and we could share the joke with our eyes every time I picked up a blue shirt. It became a great game, but it brought us closer because we gained a better understanding of what goes on inside each other's heads.

People assume just because they are married and know their partner's habits that they also know their partner's preferences and it is rare that they do. Playing a game such as this can be a wonderful opportunity to discover some of the secrets your partner may have in his/her head about likes and dislikes, turn-ons and turn-offs and where they feel they want their life to go. All of these help to build intimacy and that's well worth having in your relationship. Intimacy is all about being in the same bubble at the same time and that can happen at any time of day or night and no matter where you are. It reinforces the value of the relationship that you have with your partner.

In fact, in times when you need inner strength, you may only need to have your partner standing next to you to gain the strength that you need. The unspoken messages are what intimacy is all about. You gain this as your relationship grows, but you can also work toward it. Remember, we talked about a couple who were married for over 90 years in an earlier chapter? While you may think that people of this age may not experience intimacy, it was probably the intimacy between them that accounted for the longevity of their marriage and the happiness that was part of it. For a marriage to last that long, there had to be an element of understanding, compassion and love that is hard for most people to comprehend. However, time gives you that gift and if you stop being practical for one moment, you may actually experience it. Don't let practicalities get in the way of intimacy. Allow your partner to become part of your positive thinking process and you may just remember the intimacy that you shared so long ago, but also appreciate that you still have it in your lives.

Takeaways from this chapter:

We discussed intimacy in the broader term and tried to demonstrate what it was and what it wasn't. In case you missed salient points, this is summed up as follows:

1. Intimacy isn't how many times you make love in a week.
2. Intimacy is about sharing something so close that it's personal between you and your spouse.
3. Intimacy is being able to appreciate the same things and knowing without a shadow of a doubt that your partner is on the same wavelength as you.
4. Intimacy is about remembering all of the secrets you have shared over the years.
5. Intimacy is what happens when you allow a relationship to be encompassed by that private bubble that everyone places around themselves. When your partner is in that bubble, intimacy happens. When you decide to lock your partner out, it goes away. Anger and resentment will lock your partner out of that bubble.
6. Intimacy is understanding without the necessity for words.
7. Intimacy is knowing without the need for words.

Check out your own intimacy levels by observing how in synch your life is with your partner's life. Catch his/her acknowledgements even when they are unspoken. Feel the tingle of familiarity rather than the contempt it is able to breed.

"There's nothing more intimate in life than simply being understood. And understanding someone else." ~ Brad Meltzer

Chapter 12: Letting your Partner Spread His/her Wings

"Love entirely. Placing limitations on your love will only stunt the growth of your relationship."

~ Mulah Truth

People often place limitations on others that stop them from actually doing the things that they want to do. Clive and Eileen was one such couple who experienced the difficulties associated with limitations. As Clive got older, he found that he was unable to do a lot of the things he had done when he was younger. Marriage will go through phases such as this and the mistake that Clive made was not allowing Eileen to enjoy doing those things that would normally have been his jobs. He was trying to protect her and he could not understand her resentment until it was discussed. She felt that he was stopping her from doing things that she enjoyed, simply because he couldn't do them anymore. He thought he was protecting her from the hardship of having to do those tasks. One example was the garden. Eileen actually loved doing the gardening and all of their married life had stepped back because she hadn't wanted to take the joy away from Clive.

"He is making me old before my time" she complained and she was right. He was limiting the scope of her activities based upon what he was and was not able to do himself. In his stubbornness, he was denying her the chance to do things that he could no longer do. Instead, he insisted on employing someone to do them. Eileen was not ready to give up on life and to live a sedentary lifestyle.

During the course of a marriage, there will be changes that necessitate a different approach. For example, Jennifer was able to earn more than her husband and could supply enough cash from her job to keep their family in a fairly well off situation. However, her husband was not keen on the fact that he was being "kept" by a woman. In order to put things into perspective, Jennifer took the bull by the horns and insisted that he watched her at work to see what she was gaining from the experience. She asked her mother to babysit for the day and took her husband to the workplace so that he could see what it was that she needed out of her job. It was a job that allowed her to express herself creatively and once he saw that it presented no difficulty for her and that she was easier to live with because her creativity was catered for, he didn't mind too much that he had to stay home with the kids.

Letting your partner have freedom is vital. Do not place limitations on your partner simply because of the changing of circumstances. You need to remember that there are two of you in the marriage and that sometimes a reversal of roles is necessary as a consequence of those changes. It doesn't lessen the role that you play. In the above situation, Jennifer's husband found that there were many men who were in a similar situation, who had lost work because of company closures at an age when it was not that easy to find replacement work. He was able to watch his kids grow up and most men miss that. He was also able to learn to be adaptable and spent prime time with his wife during weekends – learning to appreciate that her previous role as mother and housewife had really been much more difficult than he had imagined.

Ambitions, hopes and dreams, keep us going. If you are able to discuss them with your partner and remember that you are both individuals with individual needs, you can make your marriage shine. One particular author friend was finding that she needed more time to write and discussed this with her husband. He was very understanding and provided her with an office so that she could have the private time needed to write her book. The book is now a success and may even be adapted into a movie and that's a great achievement. Other women have to fight for their time to do the things that they see as being more important than housework and babies. In fact, this doesn't just apply to women. A man who enjoyed meditation told me that the noise of the home was stopping him from enjoying something that he felt helped him in his high stress job. Together, they were able to come up with solutions and compromises that worked. He was able to spend money on an outbuilding for the garden, which was considered as his space for meditation.

Takeaways from this chapter:

There are several takeaways from this chapter and it was written to intentionally show that adaptations during the course of a marriage are a necessary thing.

1. This gives your partner's interests space to grow
2. It helps your partner to feel that his/her interests are taken seriously
3. It means that you gain strength as a couple, when you are able to allow your partner to try to do things that you used to consider as your tasks.

Don't clip your partner's wings by stopping him/her from trying something new. In the span of a marriage, there may be many changes. Embrace them as they strengthen a relationship, rather than weakening it.

Chapter 13: The Big Sulk

"Some people create their own storms and then get upset when it rains"

~ Anon

There is nothing worse in a marriage or a long term relationship than staying silent because you are too worried about what the reaction will be if you open your mouth and state your piece. Sulking is a relationship killer and yet adults do this all of the time because they don't want to take a conversation any further. They are, perhaps, a little afraid of what they will say because they are overwhelmed by something that has happened within the relationship. Sulking breeds unhappiness. If you are in the same room as someone that you love who is sulking, the vibrations that you get are negative. There is absolutely no doubt about it. Until they come out of that sulking session, you won't even get civility from them.

So why does sulking happen?

Sulking happens when an event provokes a reaction that seems too angry or too out of control. Thus, the recipient keeps all of his/her feelings locked up inside and doesn't react with words. They may react with veiled hints. They may react by not speaking and although this may seem very juvenile, sometimes adults do it because they don't know how to respond to something that has hurt them. Let me give you an example. Jake had to give up work because of illness. It didn't mean that he was incapable of doing things around the house. It just meant that he could not sustain this activity for a whole working day. When his wife, Ellen, came home from work, the house was always a mess. She not only had to cater for his illness, she had to bring in all of the money as well. Although they loved each other and she was capable of earning all of the money needed to keep them and to pay his health insurance, she had days when she resented it, especially when she came home and found that he had done absolutely nothing all day but play video games.

She let rip. She got angry. At the end of her tether, she let him know in no uncertain terms that she expected him to pull his weight. He was shocked by the outburst, felt sorry for himself because of his health problem and didn't know how to respond. So, for a week he sulked. He saw it as his wife's way of hurting him even more than he already was from his illness. She saw it as common sense that he needed to face up to his responsibilities. Both were justified in feeling the way that they did, but she let it out and that was a healthy approach. She could have been a little gentler perhaps bearing in mind his disability, but it was a problem that had been building up for weeks.

So how do you get past sulking?

Ellen was quick to spell it out. "I loved the guy and I didn't want to hurt him, but his continual sulking was hurting US as a relationship so I had to tackle it head on." What she did was sit in front of him so that he could see from her eyes that she was sincere. She said, "How long are you going to keep this up? We need to thrash out the problems because they are making our marriage an unpleasant place to be."

He retorted angrily that she was getting in the way of his video game, but she stuck to it. "What's more important? The video game or the marriage?" This conversation could have gone either way, but if you find yourself confronted with sulking that is making your life a misery, you need to confront it. "I am not going anywhere until this is sorted. What is upsetting you?" helps considerably to get things out into the open and discuss them. In her particular case, she was able to reassure her husband that she loved him regardless of his invalidity, but that his invalidity didn't give him the excuse to give up on her and that she deserved better than that. Once she got the message home, they were able to move forward. He learned to pull his weight and his self-esteem levels became more acceptable because he knew that there was still love there and that she would do anything to support him, provided that the feeling of respect for one another was equal.

Sulking is very destructive in a relationship. It kills off passion and it makes the ambiance of the home very difficult to live with. In fact, the old granny's tale about never going to sleep on an argument holds true to a certain extent. Making someone who is sulking face up to what's going on in his/her life breaks the ice and then, with care, you are able to piece things back together again. Sulking defies intimacy. It takes it away or makes it less important. Thus, if you have found that this has played a part in your relationship, you need to learn to handle it correctly. If you are on the receiving end, confront it and don't give up until feelings have been aired. If you are the person doing the sulking, you need to understand that harnessing your thoughts and taking it out on your loved one isn't helping anyone at all. Sulking is a little like a volcano waiting for the right moment to explode. The mental damage that it does to both of you is hard to get beyond. Thus, if you can confront these issues as and when they happen, you can kiss and make up and re-affirm your emotion for the other person without losing face. That's a much better way to go.

Takeaways from this chapter:

Sulking in any relationship is negative. If you start to feel negative thoughts about your partner, either tackle them so that they are no longer negative or look at your motives. In some cases, sulking leads to huge resentments building up that your partner may be totally unaware of, unless they are addressed straight away. If you feel that something is wrong, it's far better to address the problem, rather than let the molehill turn into a mountain. In the case described in this chapter, changes had taken place in the marriage. It meant role reversal but what had happened was that instead of cooperation, the couple distanced themselves from each other because one partner was expected to do everything and that wasn't reasonable. Had the husband in this case scenario been incapacitated to the extent that he physically could not do the tasks she expected him to, then they would have been able to look for alternatives such as home help. However, he was capable. He was just wallowing in his situation because he found it difficult to bear.

By tackling the situation, she was given the opportunity to show him that her love for him had not diminished, but that her respect for him was beginning to be affected and it was this aspect that he needed to address. Sulking makes problems bigger, rather than smaller. It creates an atmosphere between two people and may eventually erode all trust within a relationship. This should be addressed:

1. If you feel resentment, talk about it, rather than letting resentment build.
2. If you feel a frustration, let it out and become stronger as a couple.
3. Remember above all else that sharing is what marriage is all about, rather than harboring angry thoughts.
4. Sulking hurts you, but it also hurts your relationship and those close to you.
5. Sulking passes the wrong message to your children and gives them a bad example to live up to.

6. Sulking takes away the possibility of getting together and healing whatever the problem was.

If you can talk about the problems, which cause you to internalize, you are less likely to build up barriers that shut your partner out. Intimacy cannot exist when these barriers are put in place. The only way forward is to bring your problems out into the open and discuss them.

Chapter 14: And Then There Were Three

"Babies are such a nice way to start people."

~ Don Herold

When your relationship goes through all the natural stages and you find that you have a new addition coming into the family, things change. What invariably happens is that the baby becomes the focus of everyday life. It's quite a normal progression, but it can also be a period when things start to go wrong for a couple. A woman may be putting all of her energy into looking after the needs of the little one, and the man may feel left out of the picture. This doesn't always happen, of course, and some men get equally involved in the life of the baby. However, it is a danger area. You start to dress to go to bed because you know that you are going to have to get up in the night. You also start to shun each other because you are simply out of whack and tired.

Remember at all times that each of you still needs that intimacy because that's important. That means being in each other's space and being welcome. Even if it means more cuddles and less sex, that's okay because cuddles in themselves are very reassuring and your sex life will get back to what it was when things settle down a little. You need to try and remember as the child gets older that there's no need to hide your body from your loved one. You may think that it looks ugly because of the pregnancy but why not involve your husband in rubbing on the cream to help your skin to get back to how it was. Since the only reason you have put on weight is the pregnancy, he will have delighted with every change in your body and will understand that it takes time to get back to the shape that you were.

The biggest hurdle that couples face is being alone together and letting down the inhibitions. You worry that the child will need you or that a toddler will enter your room. This is something that you need to talk about. If it is causing friction between you, it's not a bad idea to keep that date night event something that you stick to, when the baby goes to grandmother and you and your spouse have a bit of grown up time together without all of these fears. You don't have to explain why you need that time together. Most grandparents will already understand, but it's important that you remember that you are still a couple. Just because one more element has been introduced, that shouldn't change the way that you feel for one another.

There are so many ways in which a child comes first. Mom may be loath to spend money on nice perfumes or things that she knows she would like. Then she feels dowdy and her husband bringing something home for her makes a welcome break from everything revolving around the baby.

Babies grow up and during the growing up stages there will be a lot to weather together. That's why the baby stages are so important. They set the scene for the next 18 years or so and that's a long time. If you stop being intimate and stop appreciating each other – concentrating only on the baby and the growing stages – there's little wonder that at the end of the day, the marriage has little substance left to it. Many couples split up after the last child has left home, but had they kept their partnership alive, there would be no need to have split up.

Date nights can take the form of a night in beside the fire, an intimate dinner together or any of the things that you used to do before the baby came along. I feel that two date nights a week is reasonable and is enough for the couple to realize that everything is okay, regardless of what chaos the new baby brings into the marriage. I also feel that it's important that the husband and wife have talked about the baby care and that this isn't just expected to become the chore of the woman. More and more men are taking their share of looking after baby and finding that this liberates them from the standard role model that actually tore couples apart emotionally for generations.

On days off from work, husband and wife need to do lots of bonding things together so that the family time is something that each enjoy, taking turns with looking after the baby so that one does not get worn out. One couple I know had a way of working out the routine whereby it fitted with their very difficult shiftwork. She was a cop and he was a doctor at the local hospital and their time at home was getting to be very difficult – like ships that pass in the night. Then they decided that they would no longer take overtime because this was eating into their relationship in a way that was detrimental. Once the overtime stopped, that allowed them to have extra time together as a family and took away a lot of the strain that they had otherwise felt.

When the baby comes along, don't let it spoil what you have. Share the responsibility, share the fun and share enough private time together so that both of you feel like you are part of a family unit, but that this is not at the expense of your love life. It doesn't have to be. Babies spell a beginning, not an end. When you find a good balance so that you are sharing the responsibility, you will find that your partner is more open to sharing intimacy and actually looking forward to it, rather than seeing it as another chore to add to her already busy schedule. It isn't easy finding the balance but it is entirely possible and many couples today are able to have kids and to still keep the passion within their marriages alive and kicking. There is a feminine side to a male character that can come out occasionally and one of the best examples of this is when it comes to caring for children and listening to their problems and helping to take the load.

Although you may joke about a man changing diapers, it's very endearing that he tries because his wife will feel that he is trying to take his share of the responsibility. That's flattering to the extreme and is very welcome by a woman who is tired from looking after energetic kids and who needs a little bit of space. Kids don't have to mean the end to anything at all. They are the beginning of a family and although the dynamics change, what shouldn't change is your attitude toward each other as a couple.

If you find that you are having difficulties after the kids are born, do talk to your partner about it. Your partner may be so busy that he/she hasn't noticed and talking about things makes it a lot easier for you to handle. If a woman is suffering from baby blues, she may also need help from a specialist but this will be worthwhile, so do try and take a little of the burden from her so that she feels free to explore this avenue. When you consider all of the hormonal changes that are taking place within her body, it's not a complete surprise that she may be going through a tough time transitioning from having a baby to being a mother.

A marriage can become very strong indeed because of children. Don't use them as the excuse for losing the passion in your marriage. You have to adjust your lives together to take account of them but also to make sure that the romance within your marriage stays intact. Giving all of your attention to the children and none to your spouse may be an error in judgment. You have to think of this as being a family unit and that includes your spouse who may be out all day earning the money it takes for your family to survive. If he comes home to a cold reception because he forgot flowers on your birthday, you need to be a little forgiving and understand that the strain of parenthood is not yours alone. It gives a great deal of responsibility to both of you.

If you can see your way through the maze and understand the new dynamics of your relationship regardless of having kids, you have a better chance of making that marriage even more solid and your love for each other deeper than ever before. Remember, if you want your partner to be there at the birth, encourage it, so that he can appreciate the difficulties of birth and can also be more sympathetic toward you when you get home.

Having children doesn't mean the end of romance. It means the beginning of something wonderful and although it may be hard to see that in the early days of sleepless nights, these do pass and you will be able to resume your love life very soon. Be honest with your partner about how you feel and work on going forward together.

Takeaways from this chapter:

You may find that life changes when the kids are born, but the intimacy and specialness of your relationship should not change. It should develop. All too often, love life is put on the back seat in favor of looking after the kids. However, in order to keep the relationship alive, you do need to remember that your partner's needs and your own personal needs should not be put off simply because there is one more member in the family. Change with the dynamics of the family, while remembering that the sexual needs don't necessarily have to change. You are dealing with adults who are also getting older. Often marriages split up because of the lack of affection shown by a spouse. However, if you take the advice given in this chapter, you will realize that your love life doesn't have to become something of less importance:

1. Your partner still needs reassurance that he/she is still perceived as being sexy.
2. You are getting older together and should always respect that your bodies are changing. This may cause a lack of self-esteem. If you let your partner know that he/she is still attractive, this can help your partner to overcome hang-ups. Your woman may have gained weight while pregnant. Let her know she is still sexy. Your man may have found his waistline has spread. He still needs to know that he is attractive. When you cut out the sexual part of your relationship, you give your partner doubts.
3. Your child should never be used as an excuse to avoid sex.
4. If your child will not allow you private time, you need to adjust your life, so that you still have adult only time in which to explore each other's bodies without having to be frightened of intrusion by a youngster.
5. Warm and contented parents whose sex lives are fulfilled make happier parents.

The child should never be an excuse for exhibiting the prudish side of your nature. Enjoy each other. You have a lifetime ahead together that needs to be enjoyable for both of you, so that you in turn can make the life of your children happier. A baby in the family is a new problem. Neither you nor your partner is accustomed to this problem. Learn to reassure each other and help each other through this period of learning because that's all it is. It should not get in the way of your relationship and if you find that it is, enlist the help of your partner so that you can get things back on an even keel.

"I am having trouble coping with the new baby" doesn't make you a bad mom. If it is the man who says this, it doesn't make him a bad father. It just means that the adjustment is harder than anticipated and it will take time and a little more understanding from you both to get you through this patch in your life. In future years, you will laugh about it, but sleepless nights and a crying baby have a habit of putting things into perspective. See it for what it is and accept it as being part and parcel of starting a family. Above all, allow your partner to feel loved, regardless of how tired the baby is making you. Chances are that your partner feels the same way and your little bit of emotional support could be all it takes to get things back on track.

Chapter 15: As Kids Get Older

"Parents were invented to make children happy by giving them something to ignore."

~ Ogden Nash

Family life will, to a certain extent, revolve around the children. As they get older, their demands get more frustrating for parents struggling to keep up with them. There's no wonder that passion dies a death. You may be worried about the next Smart phone your child is going to demand for Christmas and how you are going to afford it. You may even worry about the fact that the children are growing into little adults and trying to impose their will all of the time. However, imagine what happens when you allow the children to take precedence over your partner. The children leave home and often couples find that there is little to talk about and that much of the common ground that they used to share has been long since buried by all the worries that kids inflict on parents.

That's why it's so important to make sure that your kid's respect that you, as adults, also need to carry on doing things on your own sometimes. If you can take vacations without taking the kids, this really does give you some prime time with your partner. It shows your appreciation and it also gives you a little bit of private time together that isn't dominated by the needs of the kids. In fact, grandma and grandpa may be very happy to have the kids over for a while during the summer vacation or even during holidays that give you that chance for you and your partner to have some time together.

Although you should also have vacation time with the kids, you need to remember your own needs. These make you stronger as a couple and also mean that you are a lot more tolerant with the kids. They get to find their independence but with parents who are not afraid of their own independence as well. That means that when they ultimately leave the nest, you haven't lost touch with your personal relationship with your partner.

The kind of vacation days that you can have together are trips down memory lane or even going to places that are on your bucket list of things you want to do. If you have this in mind and can make sure that you put enough away to cater for them, rather than giving it all to the kids, the kids get a good deal out of it. They get parents who are happy together and who show them the perfect example of how marriage should work. They get parents who don't feel drained and who don't feel stressed at the thought of spending time together. They get happy parents and that's the best gift that you can ever give to your children.

What do you get out of it? You get to romance your partner all over again. Going on a cruise ship or taking to the hills together, you make your relationship stronger and you build memories that are exclusively yours. You tailor your life in such a way that you don't build up resentment and have plenty of "naughty" time together, when you don't have to play the role of mom or dad. Those roles can get wearying at times but if you manage to take that time to yourselves, you know that you always have it to look forward to and keep your romance on track.

One couple that I saw several years ago started dating each other all over again when the kids left. They had been very careful always to have time together and thus, when they reached retirement age, they were quite accustomed to sharing already. The dates that they had were at familiar places from their past. They were sentimental and the couple enjoyed going back to places where they had been and sharing very intimate memories together. Their sex life was still hot while they were in their sixties and he looked happy while she looked temptingly alluring without having to try too hard.

When you find time for yourselves, you also find that you don't forget the needs of your partner. A nice gift of a bottle of her favorite perfume tells her that you know what it is. Many couples have no idea what to give each other because they are so out of touch with their partner's needs. Similarly, how many couples do you know that scout around for ideas for Christmas gifts for their partners? I know of many and that's sad. If you keep in touch with your other half and keep a little bit of time that's yours and yours alone, you tend to share dreams more. You tend to talk more and also to listen more.

Don't let the kids become the center of your family life. Of course they need love and affection, but so does your partner and when you tackle that side of your relationship, you will be giving the kids' lives roots that are strong, so that they can go out into the world and know how to make their partner happy in the long term. Family life can be very rewarding. You get to share all the victories of the kids, but you also get to celebrate your togetherness with your partner that made all of those victories possible.

It's worth remembering that children need their space also. If you have been the type of parent who has cosseted your kids and given in to their demands, take a look at your partner and start to assess what's happened between you and him.

Takeaway from this chapter:

We have discussed how kids become the center of your attention. However, you do need to be there for each other. Some days will seem miserable if you center your whole life on the kids and do not think of yourself and your partner. Your togetherness is something that helps a child to grow up with a more balanced view of life. Yes, you will have to go through all of the growing stages of the children, although this should never make your relationship with your spouse any less important or relevant.

Exercise in togetherness

If you are the one who stays at home and looks after the kids, surprise him. Arrange that you have a weekend together without the kids. If this means sending them to their grandparents or to a friend who also has kids and who would welcome them, then do so. Start the weekend off as you mean to go on. Begin with a treat like breakfast in bed. Talk about what your partner wants to do with this weekend because chances are, he has been working hard to provide for the family and barely gets a word in when it comes to doing what he wants. He usually comes home at weekends and is surrounded by the demands of children. On this weekend, make it about him.

It takes togetherness to reap all of the benefits from a relationship. That togetherness includes doing things you both enjoy, respecting each other's wishes and giving a little extra time to your partner that they truly merit. When you do this occasionally, what you are doing is giving a clear message of "YOU are important." Sometimes that's all it needs to get your relationship back on track and if you find that your kids are hampering the closeness, this may be just what you need. Buy tickets to a show you know he wants to see. Treat him the same way as you did when you were courting and make an extra effort with your appearance. Be romantic. Let him be romantic too because this is the missing element if your home life seems to be in the doldrums.

Marriage

There's a joke in my family because my sister in law buys flowers for her husband. We all thought it was terribly amusing, though none of us knew the story that came out years after we had been teasing them about it. Apparently, the way that they met was in a garden center, looking through a patch of flowers and those flowers had become very significant for them as a couple. She wanted him to remember that day as if it was yesterday and every time she produced those flowers for him, they went through a sentimental journey together that we didn't know about. Create your own sentimental journey and see where it takes your relationship because it's certainly well worth it.

Chapter 16: Sex for the Older Couple

"A successful marriage requires falling in love many times, always with the same person"

~ Anon

During the course of your lives together, you go through all the different ages, but none gets to you as much as old age. If you are with your partner and want to rekindle that light of passion at an older age, there are many things that get in the way, but its every bit as possible. You know each other. You have a wealth of history together and you are probably quite relaxed about life. But how passionate are you? Do you go to bed in a nightdress or pajamas every night? Did you forget all about cuddles? Do you take your book to bed and get irritated when he turns over and switches off the light? Once in a while you need to show that you are still this young person inside. Don't be afraid of having fun because your partner is probably feeling the effects of age too and that's never going to be a very comfortable way to feel.

One lady that I spoke to about marriage said that once in a while, she turns up in the bedroom and shows her husband her breasts, saying something like "Yes, and I still have great breasts!" For a little old lady, it seemed kind of quaint, but when you work it out, it's no different from a man wanting to show his woman that he still has what it takes to turn heads or to be noticed by those of the opposite sex.

Don't be afraid of letting go occasionally and just doing what you want to do. For example, if you want to feel your skin next to his, why not go to bed naked? Stop conforming just because people say that's what you do at that age. You can always have your nightclothes handy in case someone knocks at the door in the morning and you want to retain your dignity. The one thing you have to remember is that you are still a couple and that means sharing fun things together that you don't share with others.

Leaving a rose on your wife's pillow can be a wonderful gesture and will light her up with a feeling that she is loved. Remember to kiss. Remember to touch. If touch is lost in a relationship, it makes it a lot harder for both of you. That touch is every bit as important as saying "good morning" is. It should be part of what you do together and be an integral part of your romance. Have you ever seen old couples dancing and holding tightly onto each other? You still get all of the feelings as you get older that you had when you were young. Men and woman can feel neglected, unloved and unsure of themselves as much as their younger counterparts. Therefore, these little shared moments of touches, kisses and tenderness help to make the relationship extra special at any age at all.

You have probably been through a lot of things together, so why not try new things and begin to laugh again. It doesn't matter that some sexual positions are a little too difficult because you are not as supple as you used to be. You can sometimes have a good laugh trying them out anyway and laughing together. It brings you so much closer and helps you to keep the romance alive.

Exercise – This is especially for older couples. Try one night of going to bed naked and see how your partner responds. Don't worry that your body isn't as lithe and lovely as it used to be. Neither is your partner's body. Feel that skin to skin and if your partner is worried about sex, let him/her know that it isn't all about sex or performance. Sometimes it's just about cuddling up together, skin to skin, and remembering all of the times that you have passed together. There's nothing nicer than knowing that your partner actually wants to share that intimacy with you, no matter whether it evolves into sex or not.

Drop the old "sorry for myself" expression when your partner doesn't particularly want sex. That makes barriers between you. It also makes men afraid to initiate again in case they get rejected. You need to learn all about the difference in the male and female psych to understand that men see themselves as the initiators. If they are rejected, they don't do very well with failure. However, there are no rules that say that she cannot initiate if she wants to. Women who do initiate don't get half as upset by rejection and will quite happily cuddle up because these are the caring partners within the relationship and it's natural for them to want to please their partner.

Instead of turning off the light, kissing each other goodnight and turning over away from each other, try kissing each other with the light on and see what sparks it brings into the picture. You will be nicely surprised that your partner is still a young person inside and that the reassurance of your kiss will be a very welcome gesture that makes your partner feel loved and needed. There's no better feeling when you are getting older than lying in bed beside someone you know has given their life to you and your family and that you have come out of the situation still loving each other. Try picking her a flower or two and never forget that sentimentality costs nothing but that it helps to keep the spark of passion alive in your relationship.

There are other ways of showing passion to your loved one. Remembering things that are special to both of you is one of those ways, especially if you are older. From out of the blue, a little comment about something that is sentimentally important to you makes you feel loved. If you can think of an event that you both enjoyed, by all means bring this up at some point but make sure that it's at a time when your partner is receptive to your comments.

You will also find that with the passing of time, your partner may go through moments on uncertainty about life. With life passing him/her by, it's not surprising that there are these moments that leave you wondering about your life. Encourage open conversation but when you do hear about your partner's fears, make sure that you listen because listening will give you a lot more clues than jumping in with reassurance. When you have heard what your partner has to say, then its time to reassure and to help your partner come to terms with whatever change is taking place in his/her life. The kind of things that come into the picture as you get older are health, loss of friends, the way that you feel inside about your femininity or masculinity and these are all part and parcel of growing older.

A woman who feels she is past her most attractive years will be reassured by a partner who is sensitive enough to her feelings to make her feel special. A man needs his wife to remind him that he is still very needed and loved and during the years when a man is losing his hair or finding that he isn't as strong as he used to be, may need reassurance that he's still the man who she loves.

Little gestures put things into perspective and help your partner to feel better about life and you needn't think that sexual contact has to stop at a set age. It doesn't. There are no rules concerning this and there are aids available for those who are experiencing difficulty. Men may be more inclined to feel sexy if it's not too late in the day when he is tired, whereas a woman may find that the introduction of gels may help with dryness. The point I am trying to make here is that although your body feels older, there's still that yearning to be loved and you should never assume that it goes away. You always remain the same on the inside, so it's quite likely your sex life can go on for years yet! It is never a sign of weakness that you need a little help. You wouldn't think twice about using a walking stick to help you to walk, so why would it be a big deal for you to use gel if it helps the sexual process? A man may even need to take tablets to help him with erections, but older people have to accept that life is like that but that the different stages of growing old should never be something that comes between them, as a couple.

Takeaways from this chapter:

Age changes things. Imagine Emmy and her husband Jimmy. He didn't talk about his problems and decided to keep them to himself. He was embarrassed. He knew that he could not perform sexually and that worried him to such an extent that he started to show very little affection for his wife, thinking that if it led to the bedroom, he would be embarrassed. What he hadn't realized was that his wife was suffering from hormonal changes that made her a little moody and things came to head one night when she actually sat up in bed, having been crying into her pillow, and confessed that she missed his affection and thought that he had stopped loving her because she was so old. On the contrary, he had stopped because he thought his own capacity to love had been impaired. This is one couple that gained a lot from talking. Both agreed on that very night that they would continue their marriage and that they would not judge each other based upon what age had done to them. She reassured him that it didn't matter whether he "performed" or not and once the anxiety was passed, he actually found that his performance was improved because of being able to drop the worry. She, on the other hand, began to feel attractive again and less shunned by her partner. She was able to stir this side of his emotions and found that it was almost like being on honeymoon all over again.

So what do we learn from this?

1. Older people may have inhibitions caused by the passing of time.
2. They may display them in a manner that looks like they don't care.
3. They may avoid physical contact if things appear to be impaired by health.
4. Talking and being aware of your partner's difficulties is essential so take time to talk and equally learn to listen.

All of these assumptions that people use as an excuse to avoid lovemaking can be overcome by conversation that is non-confrontational. Each party to the marriage has the problems associated with age to deal with, but if they discuss these with their partners, the problems become less likely to impair sexual performance. This discussion can also mean that the couple is able to share a very intimate closeness that they share with no one else. That level of sharing is very healthy and can help mend situations that seem to be insurmountable.

The passion felt by older people can actually be intensified by the passage of time. A woman who thinks she is no "spring chicken" any more may be reassured when her husband is able to talk about her sexuality. A man who is worried about his sexual performance can be reassured by a woman who loves him and accepts him for who he is, rather than how he performs! In fact, at this age, sex can be better because there is no worry about babies and once you have talked through any problems that may have arisen, you may find sexual freedom to explore each other's fantasies becomes good fun, rather than something to be worried or concerned about.

Chapter 17: The Influence of Friends

"Evil influence is like a nicotine patch, you cannot help but absorb what sticks to you."

~ Elizabeth Ann Bucchianeri

When you are married, you will still be in touch with friends and family. That's normal. But what if friendships you make are spoiling what you have at home? When you have influences that make you behave in a way that's upsetting the balance at home, sometimes it's not too obvious and, unless your partner tells you, you don't know what's happening. If you feel that any of your friends are making your marriage harder, you need to address the problem.

Carole was married for fifteen years. She was happy to go along with the interests of her husband and his friends but after a while found that she was getting bored. The reason for the boredom was the fact that she no longer got to choose the kind of things that they did together or the people who were constantly in that private living space that she shared with her husband. He had simply assumed that she was happy. The problem with this kind of scenario is that women like Carole don't actually say much. They put up with it. Their husband's friends play cards until the early hours of the morning and eat into that time which is supposed to be shared between man and wife. She felt that he was unduly influenced by them and that if he chose her over them, they would ridicule him. Thus, she didn't tell him but put up with a marriage that she found was giving her less and less of the kind of security she felt she should have.

When you have friends that are making life at home difficult, the only way to deal with it is to address the situation in a positive and upbeat way so that your partner gets the message that you want more time with him/her. For example, a woman whose girlfriends are always around the house may not be giving her husband enough individual time and he may be upset that this part of their life seems to have been taken over by her friendships.

You have to work these things out and tackle them as and when they happen. If you feel that your partner is spreading him/herself thin and doesn't contribute enough toward your intimate relationship, preferring to be with friends, nagging isn't going to cut it. You need to tempt your partner to want to be with you more. You need to perhaps make it clear that you miss his interaction with you and that you feel the marriage is getting pretty lonely without him. You may even have to suggest different ways of making sure that you get enough time together. Date nights are good for this. A date night is a night spent together without friends when you do things that you enjoy doing together. This may include getting up close and personal and making love on the rug in front of the fire, or it may involve actually going out to dinner and then enjoying conversation and intimacy. If you feel like you want your partner to yourself a little more, tempt your partner into that space you know your partner likes to be. If he is sexy, tempt him with looks he can't resist. If he likes to spend time at the theater, get tickets. If he likes to go horse riding, then arrange it. The point is that all of the things that you arrange should be things that ONLY involve you and him and that exclude the friends that have been invading your home.

Never deprive your partner of having company over or criticize his friends. It's not about competing. You are married to your spouse and they are not. Thus, you just need to get your spouse to see that time spent together is just as important as that spent with friends and do it in a way that tempts him/her rather than one that criticizes his/her choices.

Friends with bad marriages can be a bad influence on your partner. Try to balance this so that your partner sees the contrast between your marriage and that of his friends, but in a very positive way. "I really feel for Gerry that he isn't as happy as we are" in sympathetic toward Gerry but is also reinforcing to your partner that you see your marriage as being more valuable. If you were to word it in another way, you may be seen as being critical of his friend and that may not go down too well. "Your friend Garry is pathetic. He is always here. Why can't he be with his wife?" - If you say something like this, he may see you as being lacking in understanding and empathy and cold hearted.

That's certainly not the right impression to give him because he will feel alienated by your negativity.

Similarly if a man doesn't like his wife's friends being there all the time, it won't give him any brownie points criticizing them. "Good grief, your friend talks too much. No wonder her husband has left her" isn't going to make you look kind. It would be kinder to say something complimentary or kinder. "It's a shame she doesn't have more in her life. Perhaps we need to encourage her to meet a new guy" will show her that you mean well, but you need to see this friend less. However, you tackle the influential friendships within your marriage, you need to remember that you should strengthen your own position rather than use criticism and derision as tools to stop conflict. They don't stop anything and if you continue to have problems of this nature, intimacy and understanding may just walk out of the door in your relationship, leaving it every bit as sad as the marriages of friends who impose too much upon your relationship rather than getting on with their own relationships.

At the end of the day, you need to make friends who actually add something to your life. If you find that there are friendships that are getting in the way of the marriage, discuss it the moment it becomes a problem so that you can sort it out as a couple. Hayleigh and John didn't discuss their problems. She had many friends who were musical like her and she enjoyed getting together with these friends to play music. However, John always felt left out. He didn't make his opinion clear but went along to these soirees to please his wife. The problem was that because he didn't enjoy them, he always seemed miserable.

It came to a head one night when he admitted that he thought he meant less to her than her musical friends. He thought he had less to offer and this wasn't making him feel good about the relationship. Hayleigh hadn't even thought about it, but she suddenly made sense of it all. He felt left out because he was the only person in the room that was incapable of playing a musical instrument and would far rather be with people he could relate to.

They got over the worst part of the situation but it took years longer than it needed to take. If they had been more observant and more sensitive to each other's needs earlier, they could have found a compromise. In their case, the compromise was slow coming, but it was a very good one.

John took up with his gardening friends and produced wonderful produce that he was pleased to share with his wife. He became very happy and they were able to combine their interests by throwing a party for their other friends where she supplied the music and he supplied the food. That way, both of them enjoyed the company of their respective friends and were able to continue their marriage with a much deeper understanding of each other.

If you are not interested in your partner's friends, there is no need to criticize. The way to move forward is simply to state that you need friends who have a little more in common with you and find an avenue where potential friendships can be made that work for you, while letting your partner continue with friendships that are important for him/her.

My friends are not the same friends as those of my partner, although of course after all these years of marriage, we also have common friends. You need to work out which friendships are detrimental to your marriage and work out ways in which you can make those friendships work as well as keeping your partner happy and contented.

Takeaways from this chapter:

If there are outsiders who are intruding into your marriage and making things difficult, you need to address the problem:

1. Talk to your partner and be candid though try not to be critical.
2. Find alternative things you can do together, giving your partner more time with you and less with friends.
3. Learn to accept that your partner's friends are as important to him/her as your friends are to you.
4. Find compromises so that your relationship is the most important aspect and friendships fit in with your marriage, rather than adjusting your marriage to fit in with friendships.

There are various ways to do this, but you need to face the problem, work out solutions and then tackle the problems together. Don't use criticism. It helps no one. In fact, criticism may drive wedges between you. You are not to ask your partner to give up his/her friends. What you do need to make clear is that you love your partner and would like more time alone with him/her.

The problem with criticism is that it alienates your partner and may just be enough to make your partner seek comfort in the company of friends. That was never the intention and your situation can become worse than it already is. However, if you talk about things and compromise, you can save your marriage and have your friendships as well. It's simply a case of adjusting your life to make room for both, giving your partner priority since your family should always come first.

When you make angry remarks about your partner's friends, you criticize his/her choices and that's never going to be useful. Instead, work out ways in which you can continue to have friends but not let those friendships take away valuable time you and your partner need to have together, in order to be happy.

Marriage is something you shouldn't consider as being less valuable than friendships. Your partner should come first. If your partner is complaining that you spend too much time with friends, it's time to see what the real problem is. What he may be saying is that you are not spending enough time with him. Rather than taking this as an insult, addressing the situation can help both of you to become closer and to understand each other's needs.

Chapter 18: Reconnecting Outside the Bedroom

Last night, I got up the courage to ask you if you regretted us.
"There are things I miss," you said. "But if I didn't have you, I'd miss more."

~ David Levithian

The wedding was beautiful, the honeymoon left you walking on air and then you returned home to your *'happily ever after.'* Fast forward to maybe a decade later, and you are so bored, you're wondering if you married the right person, if your marriage is going to survive and how your partner went from the love of your life to your convenient roommate.

Popular media paints the picture of couples living in fairytales, with little to no real issues, a near-constant sex drive and an absolutely fluffy, happy life together. As I already mentioned earlier – don't go into marriage with these expectations. They are not real, and they will last as long as the honeymoon itself. And then you will crash down to Earth hard and fast. Remember that it's not about whether you married *'The One,'* but how you can make it work with the one person you have tied yourself to for all eternity.

To that extent, what matters is rekindling the romance between you. In the early days, it was about discovering one another, figuring out what made the other tick and then building a life together. Now, it is about *re*discovery and keeping that life stable and fresh, despite having been together for more years than you care to count. When kids come into the picture, you barely have any time for each other and so you end up taking one another for granted, foregoing your *"please"* and your *"thank you" attitude,* because hey, what does one thank you matter when you're rushing to get to work on time after dropping your son/daughter off at school?

And that's where the problem begins. Other than your usual miscommunication and misunderstandings, most marriages start tanking when you take the little things for granted. I'm not saying that you have to be perfect – that's a ridiculous notion, not to mention impossible. What I *am* saying is that the resentment builds up over time, when the little things get ignored, and then boil over into one big, messy fight that leaves both of you scrabbling for purchase.

All this may seem like generic advice, but what I am saying is that you need to start dating again. You need to recapture that old sense of excitement and romance and begin enjoying one another the way you used to, instead of automatically assuming that your partner is going to always be there. He/she will be there, of course, but that doesn't mean that you can't let them know how much you appreciate them! So here are some things you can do daily to reassure your partner that you no longer take them for granted.

- Your old passionate kisses have now morphed into those sweet, domestic pecks; it is cute, in theory, but occasionally surprising your spouse with a passionate kiss can let them know just how important they are to you. When you get home from work, push aside your tiredness long enough to kiss your partner hard on the mouth and let them know that they were missed during the day.
- Do not forget the three magic words – and I don't mean just '*I love you.*' Saying that you love your spouse is important, though you also need to tell your spouse, '*please*', '*sorry*' and '*thank you*' when he/she deserves it. Just because you have made the commitment to build a life together, it doesn't mean that you can let go of these common courtesies. So when Casper picks up the dry cleaning for Deanna, she thanks him, both verbally and with a passionate kiss – it works! A little appreciation goes a very long way.
- Look after your appearance. Remember those days when you women would put on extra lipstick or you men would slap on some sexy cologne to impress your partner? Bring those days back. I'm not saying you need to look like a million bucks every day, but take the time to make yourself look nice. Not only will your partner approve, you will feel more confident about yourself. Feeling good about your own personality will go a long way in getting rid of any pent-up resentment.
- Have your relationships outside of the marriage. When you begin to depend too much on one person, you may end up suffocating their sense of independence or individuality. Have friends

outside and plan a weekend out with – swapping stories and trading anecdotes worked for you when you were dating, they will work now too!

- Have an active sex life and pursue your *own* pleasure as much as your partners. The next chapter focuses on reconnecting between the sheets, but as a precursor, I'd like to tell you that it is not wrong to be selfish in the bedroom. Media tends to romanticize the whole idea of giving your partner pleasure – you should, definitely. But in ignoring your own pleasure, you do yourself disservice. You may subconsciously even build up resentment towards your partner without knowing it. Enjoy what you do between the sheets and don't be afraid to chase your own fun as much as your partner's!

- Every night, before you go to bed, whisper a single praise for your partner into their ear. It doesn't have to be something big, it doesn't have to be life changing. Just whisper one good thing about them that touched you that day, and they will reciprocate. It will make you feel good about one another and you will go to sleep with a smile on your face.

- When you criticize your partner, you're very specific about the things they do that irritate you. Deanna screams at Casper for throwing his socks about the room like a slob. But when you praise them, you tend to be very generic, like, *"You're the best thing that ever happened to me."* That's nice, but it gets boring after a while and begins to feel forced – like you're saying it because you *have* to, and not because you mean it. So be specific in your praise. In what way is she/he the best thing to happen to you? Instead of that, Deanna can tell Casper, *"You make my heart race every time you kiss me."* It makes him feel good and he'll take that into account the next time he kisses her.

These are those everyday little things you can do to try and let your spouse know how much you appreciate them. Once you get into the groove of things, you yourself will be able to figure new, small ways to express your affection for your partner, like keeping dinner ready for when they return or helping them wash the car.

Apart from the day-to-day activities, what you need to do again is to go on dates. Now, most couples will protest – *'we already go on date nights, and still we find it hard to reconnect!'* The problem is *that* you go on date nights. The dates have become so much a part of your schedule and routine that they have contributed to the boring rut you have fallen into, instead of bringing you out of it. Added to that is the fact that you stick to the same old routine again and again – dinner at a fancy restaurant or a movie together. Remember when you were dating? You didn't blow money at a fancy, upscale place every week! It was fun just going out for something as simple as an ice cream, because you went *together*. It is that romance you want recapture.

Spontaneity accounts for a whole lot in any relationship. Of course, when you have kids, it can be difficult – you can't leave them unsupervised and you need to plan and organize your schedule around theirs. But at the same time, you can't afford to let yourself fall into a mindless routine that has you bored beyond comprehension – you and your partner need to spruce things up and try something new. Not only does this help you reconnect, it will also give you a sense of accomplishment and boost your self-confidence that will make you feel much better about yourself.

So, on a random evening, call up a babysitter or call your neighbor to watch your kids and then whisk your partner away for something fun. As I said earlier, you take fun for granted in the face of responsibilities – you forget to live in the moment, and bump spending time together down to the bottom of the list. Go do something enjoyable – something you haven't tried before, like going to the theatre or going ice-skating.

Here are some fun things to do together that will help you reconnect –

- ***Arts and crafts*** are always a fun way of reconnecting. Ceramics and painting, in particular, can be extremely seductive; you start out by having fun together and the next thing you know, you're getting hot and heavy between the sheets! You only need to watch the movie "Ghost" to see this kind of seduction in motion.
- ***Go exploring***. You don't have to go on a vacation; leave the kids with a trusted sitter for the day and leave behind all gadgets except your phone – which is to be used *only* in emergencies! Pick a part of your city or town you haven't been to before, switch off your GPS and then just walk around that neighborhood arm-in-arm. Or if you enjoy the outdoors, try hiking in the nearby forests or walking along unexplored parts of the beach. Remember

that joint exploration means joint shared experiences and this gives you loads to talk about when you mull over the photos. You also get to experience different people and places that help you to stay on the same page as your spouse.

- ***Take a dance class together***. Tango and waltz are good ideas – they're fun to do and they can act as seductive precursors to passion. You don't have to be perfect in learning the skill – the idea is to spend time together and have fun together again, like you used to. Perhaps it's a good time to get up close and personal and do some "dirty dancing."

- Go to a ***comedy club or watch a play*** together. These things are fun and allow you to connect intellectually like you used to – instead of discussing family finances or the kids' education plans, you can reconnect and speak of your own interests and hobbies like you haven't since your early days together. It may be a play you have been looking forward to seeing or even an act in the local bar. It doesn't matter. It's a shared experience.

- ***Go stargazing or cloud-gazing together.*** It is cliché, it is romantic and it is absolutely free. Many times, couples put off 'dates' due to financial constraints; this is one good date you can enjoy together without an expense whatsoever. Have a late night picnic, lie on the ground and pick out random patterns from the sky – on stars or clouds. Don't be afraid of looking silly – that's the point! Enjoy your time together and laugh out loud. You may not have to venture further than the back garden, but that will give your neighbors something to talk about.

- Go to a public place and then **do some people watching**. This is actually a fun way to connect – make up crazy stories about the people you see, as though you were a writer. You could even start off the story and have your partner continue it – the silliness of it will make you smile and laugh together in ways you haven't in a long time. Airports are great for this as is the street café in the local mall.

- **Be kids**. When you rake leaves together, make a huge pile and jump into them. It isn't just the kids who deserve to have fun, after all! Make it a family affair, instead – get your partner to join in and throw up leaves in the air together. Don't be afraid to have *fun* – responsibility will keep for an hour or two and your kids will appreciate the time with their parents. Try skimming stones. One of you will do it better than the other and that gives you something to be competitive about. Try it; it's fun.

- **Read out loud to each other.** You put your kids to sleep by reading to them fun stories and making fun noises. Why not try the same with your partner? Only, instead of reading *Dr. Seuss*, you might want to try something like *Fifty Shades of Grey*, which will get you going in the bedroom! On a more serious note, sometimes just reading each other to sleep can be quite romantic and intimate.

- **Take long showers or baths together**. In the hurry of your everyday lives, you've quite forgotten how much fun it can be to take a hot shower together. In fact, doing it without the possibility of sex actually increases the intimacy – you trust your partner to take care of you the way you would look after yourself. Washing your partner can be an incredibly humbling as well as erotic experience, so try it! It doesn't matter if you sink their rubber duck. In fact, it can be part of the fun. Try soaping each other up and blowing bubbles. It's fun and it's free and it makes bath time a little less of a chore and something for you to look forward to.

- ***Do chores together.*** This sounds boring – but it really isn't! Instead of nagging each other to get things done, when you do it together, you have fun together and you can communicate. The chore isn't boring anymore, it gets done faster and it allows you to connect to each other again. You're both working at the same time, so any resentment one feels over the other not doing enough fades away. Plus, throw in some fun music – maybe rock or pop – and you can jive while vacuuming or cleaning the kitchen and have fun together! The way to introduce this is when you know that you have guests coming over to your house. Tell your partner it's time to clean up ready for the guests and each take your turn doing what needs doing. You may find your partner is better at cleaning up the kitchen than you are!

- ***Work out together.*** You get healthier together and exercising as a couple can be quite the seductive game. Couples tend to stick to fitness programs if they do it together – they can motivate each other and it's fun and exciting. By the same token, it you are dieting, why not do the diet together and both benefit from it? It makes it much more fun and gives you the impetus to keep the diet up, even on those days when you don't feel like it.

Whatever you do, do it *together*. What you need to do is to spend time *with* each other like you haven't since the early days of your relationship. Somewhere along the way, you began to ignore each other and that has damaged the level of intimacy you share. The love you had for one another is still there, though it's faded into a light glow instead of the bright, passionate flame it used to be. You have to rekindle it.

When you do fun things with someone, you tend to associate the idea of fun with that person. Given that you and your partner haven't done anything 'fun' together in a long time, your marriage has begun to seem boring to you. So do fun things with your partner, instead of speaking to him/her about only the responsibilities you share. Don't just go for the usual Saturday movie or dinner with friends – that's good, yes, but it's hardly fun or exciting.

Most often, with adults, the problem lies in the fact that we don't want to appear silly or stupid in front of others. Children don't have that inhibition – they enjoy themselves fully and completely, laughing out loud and living in the moment. Learn to do that with your partner – it doesn't matter if you do something silly or stupid, as long as both of you are having fun together again. Go back to the place where you first met and reminisce – it will allow to you to remember why you married him/her in the first place.

And the cardinal rule of re-dating – *don't talk about the kids, the family finances or any responsibilities you have.* The occasional comment on them is all right, but don't let your entire discussion revolve around those topics – you speak of them enough at home, you don't need it now too! The point is to *reconnect* – rediscover your old interests, find some new ones and see what your partner thinks. Get to know one another again.

Another good idea is to try out things that frighten you. For instance, Casper is afraid of going on the roller coaster, since he has a fear of heights. So when he and Deanna are trying to reconnect, a good idea is for them to go to the amusement park and try the roller coaster. As they are in the park, Casper will cling to Deanna the closer they get to the ride. They physical contact will reaffirm their connection to one another. He will probably hang on to her through the entire ride itself – at the end of it, he will come out smiling and laughing, because he overcame his fear and he remembered that she was there to hold him up the way she always had been.

When you do something you have always been afraid of, you get a sense of accomplishment and confidence. It is actually a scientific process – a chemical called dopamine is released in your brain that makes you feel really good about yourself. This chemical is also released when you start falling in love with someone; what you're essentially doing now is combining both scenarios – from now on, you'll associate the giddiness you felt overcoming your fear with your partner, which will reaffirm your relationship with them.

As you keep doing fun things together, you will slowly see that the good feelings from your dates bleed over into your normal, everyday lives. Don't stick to one specific day a week for your dates – change up your schedules a little. Don't stick to one pattern of dating; try new things and new places. Take turns planning it out and don't let your partner know what you're doing – the surprise adds another enjoyable element to the whole experience! Above all, have fun together. The new memories you make will be precious – they will also provide more things to talk to one another and your friends about. The dates will keep you entertained even after it's over. When was the last time you discussed your Saturday movie? But a fun ride at the amusement park where you overcame your chronic fear of heights is always something to recount, even make into a lesson for when your kids are trying to overcome their fears!

The good feelings will have a lasting effect on you and your relationship. You will slowly begin to appreciate your partner more and it will be reciprocated in the small things they do for you. Remember, grand gestures last only for a couple hours, but the little things – like telling your partner to *'have a great day!'* or kissing them passionately when they walk in can make the difference between a successful and a failed marriage. If your husband is looking especially good that day, then make sure to tell him so. If your wife makes a tasty dessert for you, then be sure to thank her for it. Let your partner feel appreciated and have fun together – that can go a long way in reestablishing the old bond between you.

There's a lot more to marriage than domestication. You need to recapture all of the elements that were there in the relationship at the beginning. Excite each other sometimes. Surprise each other and keep something up your sleeve so that you can surprise him/her again and again because these wonderful moments are what keep the marriage fresh and new. Some couples do silly things like leaving notes in lunch boxes or under the pillow. There's nothing wrong with this. What you are doing is building up a lifetime of positive experiences to make the marriage fresh and new all of the time, regardless of the monotony of responsibilities that you both have toward each other. Marriage should be just responsibility. It needs to be a fun experience as well.

I looked across the room at my partner a few moments ago. As I did so, I winked. I did it in a very deliberate way and my partner's eyes lit up. Stop taking each other for granted. Surprise each other in nice ways. That wink cost me nothing, but it brought some goodwill into our day. In the same way, you will have small ways in which you can show your partner that the love is still very much alive and kicking. That's when relationships blossom and grow. Although they may not have the same amount of passion as they did when they started, the passion and intimacy of a long-term relationship can be even better.

If you can reconnect with your partner outside of the bedroom, then that's a great start. It means that you are letting your partner know that you respect the things that he/she wants to do in their lives and are willing to become a part of those hopes and dreams. Sharing hobbies and interests also firms up the relationship and gives you something in common to talk about other than just family. You need that. You need to be able to connect on a personal level and have things to talk about that keep your relationship vibrant and happy.

For example, if he always wanted to learn photography, there's nothing wrong with encouraging it and sharing the interest. With so much available to everyone in this day and age, you need to look at what's missing in your relationship and fix it. If he takes up a hobby that doesn't include you, there's nothing wrong with taking the time to admire what he has done. Similarly, if a woman takes up a hobby that doesn't include the man, often compliments and care from their partner seems to be the missing element. You can do things independently and together but as long as you come back together and share all of your discoveries, it keeps the relationship from going stale.

I remember a friend of mine wanted to become a writer and thought that his wife would laugh at the idea. I talked to her on another day about something else and mentioned how important it is that people are able to do the things within their lifetimes that they feel passionate about. We mentioned writing and it was really strange. She looked quite distant for a moment and then said "Ah yes, I remember when I was courting Stanley. He always wanted to write. I wonder if he does now. Perhaps I could get him a computer all of his own so he can try." Although it took this conversation with friends to get her on the right track, they really did enjoy what happened after this. He became a published writer and she enjoyed showing off his work to her friends because she was proud of his achievement.

Never take all the limelight for yourself in a marriage. The fact that you can do something is because the relationship allows it to be done. Many people live in restricted lives where they don't ever seem able to do things that matter to them because responsibility gets in the way. If you can put aside biases and preconceived ideas that you have about your partner and embrace their new interests, you may find that you are opening up the possibility for your partner to feel passionate about something and that often rubs off in your romantic life too! Think back over your relationship and remember what dreams and hopes you both had in the early stages of the relationship. Re-awaken the interest and let it happen.

The relationship has changing dynamics all of the time and you can cash in on these to show your partner what he/she means to you. If your partner shows an interest in something that you feel you would like to try too, why not surprise your spouse by booking up a course that you can take together? It's not about being competitive although than can be fun too, but it's about finding out the things that you both enjoy and making those interests part of your life. One particular couple who came for advice had a joint interest in flea markets and they were able to build on their marriage by going out every week to see what bargains they could find. He was redundant and was feeling that he contributed nothing to the marriage, though in a short space of time was able to start making money from home by using eBay and proving to his wife that the things he bought at flea markets and garage sales had a good value to them. In fact, they both took up the same activity in the end and would take in turn wrapping up the parcels. Their earnings helped them to pay for a holiday that they had been promising themselves for years.

If you can find what floats your partner's boat and find a way that you can share it, then you are onto a winner, especially if this is something you can both feel passionate about. It brings you closer together and your mutual interest in activities is something that really does strengthen the marriage.

Takeaways from this chapter:

In this chapter, we have emphasized re-connecting and this is vital to keep your relationship alive. We have mentioned about the niceties that couples need to remember when dealing with their loved one. These are the ways in which one partner communicates with another. Again the emphasis is on the following:

1. Mutual respect for each other
2. Appreciation of each other and of the role played by the other party
3. Remembering interests and being prepared to share them
4. Expecting trust but giving the same amount of trust in return

If you think of your partner as being a very special part of your life, you automatically include your partner in your plans and dreams in life. You don't cut your partner out of those things that interest you. You also have to appreciate that your partner's interests are not always going to be the same as yours. Give and take is essential and there is nothing wrong with pursuing your own interests, provided that this is not at the cost of the relationship.

We also talked about reconnecting in a romantic way, remembering all of the things that attracted you to your partner in the first place. Alison forgot all of these elements. She began to nag her husband. She began to only see the negative side of his character, until her husband could no longer face another day of negativity. She would not admit that she had a problem and made no attempt to save her relationship, although her negativity was as a result of her own problems, rather than anything he had done. She walked out of the relationship but walked straight into another relationship that ended up going in the same direction. Be positive. See the positive side of your relationship and stop seeing everyone else's grass as being greener. It isn't. It is simply the way that two people connect that keeps the relationship alive. If you choose to introduce negativity, don't be surprised if your partner gets tired of it. On the other hand, try handing out a compliment from time to time and introduce positivity and you will find that you can rekindle your relationship and continue to get a great deal of pleasure from it.

If a child is constantly criticized and fed negativity, that child will rebel. A husband or wife who loses the positive connectivity with his/her partner because of negativity will react in the same way. Reconnection will stop this from happening. See the cup half full instead of always finding flaws.

Chapter 19: Learning to Deal with Inhibitions

"Happiness is a risk. If you're not a little scared, then you're not doing it right."

~ Sarah Addison Allen

During the course of any relationship, there are parts of you that you want to keep private. In a marriage, when you are living under the same roof as the person that you love, it's harder to hide inhibitions. Besides anything else, if you are able to share these and work your way through them together, you bond in a much closer fashion.

Don't like making love with the light on? You can overcome this one by talking about it with your loved one who will probably give you reassurance and who will want to see you naked. It's a real turn on for a man to see a woman's body and even if you are only willing to work through this inhibition a little bit at a time, you will find that you will get an awful lot closer with your man if you can drop inhibitions. You may say that you are worried about your tummy bulge or perhaps you don't have the best breasts, but your man didn't marry you for what your body looks like. His body will have changed over the course of the relationship as well, and there may be areas that you can help him with. The key here is to trust your partner not to criticize you. When this trust is lost, it's very hard to get it back.

Let's look at some common inhibitions that people have and you may find that these relate to you or your partner. All inhibitions are related to anxiety of some kind so you need to recognize and address that anxiety if you want to overcome the inhibition.

Women –

Women may act like the lady in bed because they have been brought up by people who have instilled values that they consider normal for women with any kind of self-respect. The problem is that if a man has a certain image of what his lady should do or be comfortable with, it's hard for a woman to know what's acceptable. They may be against the following kinds of behavior:

- Oral sex
- Masturbation
- Doing a striptease for their loved one
- Initiating sex
- Trying new sexual positions

It's hardly surprising that women think in this way when so many messages are given to them during the course of growing up, by parents who wish to keep their daughters safe from harm. The trouble is that sometimes the advice that girls are given by their parents sticks and goes into adulthood as being the normal way for girls to behave. That causes inhibitions that a woman may find it hard to break. With a little coaxing however and a lot of open discussion a couple can overcome these problems and make it easier for her to try different things that she may otherwise never experience. She may even get to like some of them. It's getting a little easier for women to discuss these subjects, although some women avoid them because they are afraid that their man will think them "forward" for mentioning things that men are supposed to think about! If you are a woman who worries about things like this, you can introduce things into the bedroom by explaining to your man that what happens in your bedroom is something special between you and him and that no rules should apply that will end up in judgment of some sort. Ask your loved one if you can talk about something and follow their reaction because most men will be only too happy to discuss sexual matters with their partner.

Men

Men may also have inhibitions caused by experiences they had during puberty:

- Size of penis
- Being seen naked
- Worry about not being able to sustain erection

- Lack of imagination to try different positions – and indeed fear of failure

If you add all of this inexperience together, it's the recipe for disaster as far as bedroom etiquette goes. If one or other of you has inhibitions, these will be very hard to break, but it is possible if you follow the details shown in this chapter. They have been written from the experience of many couples that have also had all of these problems and may help you to overcome any inhibitions that you may have. When you consider the ignorance of men to actually be aware of what part of the female anatomy achieves orgasm, as displayed on a YouTube video, it's hardly surprising that many women do not actually have orgasms. Instead of embarrassing their men, what they tend to do instead is actually fake orgasm by making appropriate noises in the right place. That's okay short term, but what about long term? You can only keep up that kind of action for a certain amount of time before you start questioning "what's in it for me?" If it isn't addressed, the woman ultimately makes love as a duty rather than a pleasure and that's a real shame for her and for him, when with a little explanation and understanding, their sex lives could actually be very satisfying indeed.

Dealing with the anxiety

If you feel that there is some kind of inhibition in your bedroom, share this chapter with your partner. Your partner may be a little afraid of exploring the potential of expanding the love making potential, but if you show him/her that you want to do this together, it's less likely that it will be seen as criticism of any kind. Remember that criticism is exactly what he/she will be afraid of and if you add this to the menu, don't expect to actually overcome the inhibition problems. Remember, these are deep rooted anxieties that may have been a part of your loved one's life for a very long time. Unless you know where the anxiety came from, you can't really understand it. For example, someone who has been in an abusive relationship may be shy about lovemaking because of that abuse and needs to feel safe with you.

Talk about safety above all else, because this may help to alleviate the anxiety side of things. If you approach this from the point of view that you are going to be spending all of your life together and should try as many different things as possible to keep the spark in the relationship, then there's nothing wrong with this approach. One of the first class ways of finding out what turns your partner on, is discussing what his/her fantasies are, but remember that if you go into this, you must not be judgmental. You may be very surprised that your partner has a lot of fantasies but has never discussed them because they are just that – fantasies. If you encourage your partner to share these, assure your partner that there will be no judgment, but that you think it would be nice to know what turns your partner on. You may find that there are actions that you take that your partner finds rather sexy. You may even have clothing that your partner finds sexy and that doesn't necessarily mean sexy attire. Woman can be extremely turned on by the smell of a freshly ironed cotton shirt on a man and that's hardly X rated. Similarly, a man may find that certain clothing outlines parts of her anatomy that he finds tempting and tantalizing.

Then talk about what turns your partner off. This is also important to know. If you have been chewing at her ear and she hates that feeling, chances are that she has put up with it because she doesn't want to hurt you, but supposing that nibbling her nipple gives her much more joy, wouldn't you rather be doing that? You need to talk openly but there's something else that you need to inject into your bedroom talk. In normal circumstances, women are expected to behave in a certain way. They will have been taught ways that are acceptable to behave in public. What she needs to know is that in the privacy of the bedroom or within your lovemaking acts, she doesn't need to adhere to those strict rules at all because this is a special place where what happens between you is intimate and is yours and yours alone. Encourage open dialog and when it happens, keep judgement out of the picture. If your wife is turned on by men with beards, don't immediately jump on the fact that the postman has a beard and accuse her of things that may make her regret she told you. When you open up and tell your loved one about sexual things, judgement should never form part of the picture. Your loved one is sharing something extremely intimate and if you judge him/her because of the truths you are hearing, your partner may decide that it isn't worth confiding in you and that's going in the opposite direction.

If you don't know how to start a dialog with your partner, wait until a time when you and your partner are both relaxed and introduce the texts of the Kama Sutra or a book on different sexual positions because that way, the information you are learning together is from a book and you won't leave doubts in your partner's mind that you picked up ideas from a former lover. That will always be something that will be frowned upon. Women have a decided disadvantage. They are supposed to be the submissive ones, although in this day and age, all of that is changing. Watch a movie like 50 Shades of Gray and discuss how your partner feels about that kind of sexuality. Whatever you use to open a dialog with your partner, be open to his/her ideas and remember that criticism is not to form part of the discussion. This is the bedroom. If you want things to be hot between you, you need to get past your inhibitions if you want to discover each other's potential as lovers.

Setting the scene

Agree to talk about intimate things and make sure that the moment chosen is one when both of you can give the other their full attention. Never start something like this with a serious statement like "We need to talk" as this may give the wrong message. Try opening it with something like "I think we can explore more sexual things together. Want to try?" as that's optimistic and shows promise. You could even have some books on positions or even a light porn film if you think that it covers an area you know to be something you both have problems with. Make the bedroom very welcoming. You can even introduce candles to make the room even sexier and take a bath together before the main event if that's what you enjoy. Taking a shower together can work as well. If your partner has come in from work and is taking a shower, what's to stop you stripping off and joining your partner, soaping your partner's body and enjoying the nakedness of the moment?

Opening up a dialog

For this to happen, you have to have an idea of where you want the conversation to go. How about opening with talking about your partner's fantasies and taking it from there. You may be surprised that your partner is thoroughly sick of the Missionary position and wants something a little more adventurous. To make this even more interesting, you could think of the whole talk as being something that needs the same lead up as sex:

- Foreplay or tease
- Pleasing each other
- Learning about the body

The foreplay in this sense means the dialog that you have between you. For example, you can ask your woman where she likes to be touched. A man can also tell his woman where he likes to be touched and what turns him on. It isn't a question of just jumping into bed and making love. Take your time and talk about things that matter to you. When exploring each other's bodies, talk about what feelings your partner gets when you do certain things. Take ideas from your books or from your porn movie and try them out for yourself. The clue here is that whatever you talk about remains in the bedroom or at least between the two of you. There has to be that level of trust or it won't work. If a woman feels that she will be teased about something that happened in the bedroom, she may be less likely to try new things.

If the woman is nervous about being seen in the nude, reassurance helps, as does light that is dimmed and more romantic and that makes her body look great. For a man, if he has problems because of inexperience, there's nothing wrong with trying different things and finding out together which touch makes him feel sexier. If he has inhibitions about climaxing too early, reassurance from his woman will help because the less the anxiety, the more able he is to perform for longer. It's the anxiety itself that may be making things difficult for him. If you find that your lover is disappointing, don't blame it on the way that he is because it won't be a permanent thing and could be related to stress. If you take the stress out of the picture, his performance may improve vastly.

Pleasing each other is what lovemaking is all about and knowing the different parts of the body that give each of you pleasure will help in this. It may not always be in the bedroom, but a kiss on the back of the neck sometimes can say an awful lot and can really make someone feel loved, if indeed that's something that particular person enjoys.

Learning about the body and how the body responds to different touch will also help you to keep this part of the marriage vibrant and meaningful. There are those who argue that it's not easy to keep the sexual part of a relationship active over the whole course of a lifetime, but love is what it's all about and if you can learn to comfort each other and help each other to overcome inhibitions, then that really will help you to understand how your partner ticks and for your partner to understand what makes you tick.

There are several ways of approaching the subject of sex but the best way is to wait until you are both relaxed and in the mood. When something happens that is predictable, why not change your position and talk to your partner about your fantasies. Everyone has them. Watching a movie together like 50 Shades of Gray may open up a dialog between you so that you can talk about things that you have never done before, but want to. Perhaps you want to be dominated in bed. Perhaps you want to dominate. However, before you play these games, let your partner know that it's just for fun and that you love him/her just the way that he/she is, but think that you can make things even more fun by being totally honest with each other.

If you haven't tried tantric sex, you haven't lived! The whole idea of tantric sex is not your own pleasure although that will happen. It's all about giving pleasure to your loved one and making your loved one the focus of your lovemaking and massage. The idea of Tantric sex dates back to before Christ and you may be surprised to know that books written on the subject were actually written by Monks for a very good reason. They wanted people to be happy within their marriages and the Kama Sutra was one such book written to give direction to people who may otherwise have had very little experience of sex or oneness.

With tantric sex, you give everything that you have to pleasure your partner and there's nothing wrong with that. They, in return, get their turn to pleasure you. The use of massage oils is very sensual indeed and can really spice up your love life, but do make sure that you protect your sheets! Take a bath together and prepare yourself for something so intimate that there are no inhibitions. Discuss the rules first if you want to and the only real rules are there nothing is banned unless your partner has a particular aversion that makes them feel very uncomfortable. Some men don't like the scrotum area being massaged as this is a very sensitive area and they are afraid of being hurt. Similarly, some women are not keen on having their anus played with. As long as you set the rules first, you can keep within those guidelines so that both of you are comfortable with the experimentation that you are experiencing. You will also find out all of the areas of your partner's body that give him/her pleasure. Inhibitions are something that you can work around and letting your partner know where you want to stop will enable you to experiment more and enjoy your intimate time together.

Takeaways from this chapter:

There are certain ways of approaching sex that open up a dialog. Criticism is not among them. If you feel that your partner is a little nervous or has anxiety problems when it comes to bedroom etiquette, then you need to encourage them in the following ways:

1. Open up conversation at an appropriate time, without leveling criticism.
2. Read books together and try fun experiments with sex just for the fun of it.
3. Talk about your inhibitions and try to work your way through them.

There is no room in the bedroom for belittling your partner and when you approach the subject of sex, you need it to be at a time when your partner is receptive to your overtures. For example, if your partner has worked hard and is too tired, this isn't the best time to try experimenting because he may feel obliged to live up to your expectations and that's not fair when he has been working all day and is really too exhausted. Choose times when you are both relaxed.

Never force your ideas on your partner. If you do, you are encouraging negative thoughts in your partner's mind about whether or not you believe they satisfy your sexual cravings. If a man believes he is not living up to the expectations of a woman, this will make him recoil rather than experiment and enjoy. Thus no criticism should be leveled at your partner and your approach should always be open and engaging.

We learned about different types of sex and about discussing any problems that you have with your partner. If your partner does not know that you don't like being touched in a certain way, it's time to make that clear in a good way and to show your partner where you like being touched.

By going through all of the different aspects of sex with your partner, you are able to keep the spark ignited. Keep your partner interested and remember that it's in your own interests as well because the more satisfied your partner is, the more satisfaction you gain as well as gaining confidence and experience. In the next chapter, we are covering those things that are best avoided if you want your love life to be more active. Of course, in a sensitive area such as this, you need to be aware of your partner's inhibitions and their boundaries. For the time being, explore these together so that you know your partner's likes and dislikes and your partner is familiar with yours.

Chapter 20: Knowing Which Buttons to Avoid

"To be trusted is a greater compliment than being loved."
~ George MacDonald

With any relationship, no matter how close, there will always be things that you need to avoid in order to keep the relationship harmonic. One of the mistakes that people make, and couples in particular, is to keep bringing up things that have happened in the past and that ruins a relationship. If your marriage appears to be going stale, then you need to really look into it and find out why. There are certain behavioral traits within a relationship as close as this that involves total trust. If you remind your partner of his/her mistakes all the time or when things go wrong, you are showing your partner lack of trust. This element of trust is essential to a relationship and it's important that you remember that.

In fact, if you think over the course of your marriage, you will probably find those buttons to avoid and these are ones that really do betray you and make your loved one feel that betrayal as well. Perhaps she used to go out with a friend in the old days. Stop reminding her of it. All you are doing by rubbing it in is showing your own inadequacies and that's not healthy for the relationship. Who did she marry? If you have made mistakes during the course of the marriage, then you wouldn't expect her to keep bringing these up and embarrassing you.

The no-go areas for couples that really do want their relationship to work are these:

- Comparison with past loves
- Criticism in a very personal way
- Criticism of looks
- Criticism of the way situations are handled

I have cringed when I heard a man criticizing his wife and telling her that the hair appearing on her chin was making her unfeminine. The fact was that she had gone through a lot of hormonal changes and these were a consequence. It made her feel bad every time that he mentioned them and it really was an unkind thing to do. Imagine if she had done the same kind of thing to him after having chemotherapy! It isn't kind and it's too personal to be an acceptable way to behave. She actually mentioned to me that the problem with dealing with the hair was the fact that her eyesight was a little defective, so he should have been more sympathetic in his approach.

There are always going to be no go areas in any relationship and if you want your relationship to last, it doesn't mean being dishonest and telling your partner that he/she looks great when he or she doesn't. It just means being more discreet and being more aware of all the changes that are happening in his/her life.

Similarly, a man may go through personal things as well. A woman needs to be supportive and loving. In fact, both sexes need to be aware that life sometimes throws curve balls and the way to keep a relationship fresh and vibrant isn't to pick on weak points caused by circumstances.

When Susan and James walked into the marriage guidance counselor's office, they both felt resentment. She was fed up of being compared to his ex-girlfriends and he was fed up with having a wife who appeared not to care about her appearance. What the counsellor did was get them to concentrate on each of their strengths rather than keeping harping on about differences.

James learned that his wife was losing confidence in herself and, as a result, was not as caring about her appearance as she had been in the past. He also found out that it was his criticism that was triggering this insecurity that caused her self-esteem issues. He also learned that it wasn't a good idea to compare her and that comparison is always cruel and is a no go area in a marriage. He was truly sorry for the damage that he had caused her and as he gave her more and more support, the couple was able to make their marriage a lot stronger. Not only did he walk away from counseling sessions feeling rather sheepish about his criticism of his wife, but James also learned to be a better person in the process. As for Susan, she learned to stop bottling up her feelings to the point of crying.

She had done this in the past because she didn't feel she could talk about them, having already been criticized for everything and didn't want more criticism added to the picture. She was equally guilty in a way because she had been keeping all of her feelings inside and had stopped really confiding in her husband. Once they regained that total trust, they were able to move forward in their marriage and make it work better than it ever had done in the past.

It's always going to be important to recognize what things are harmful to your loved one and for those who internalize their feelings, they need to learn to confide, to cry when they need to and to let out those feelings so that their partners have a better understanding of what's going on inside them.

Jim and Sally had problems in their marriage and they were not sure where the problems were coming from. Every time that Sally tried to get close to Jim, he appeared to be backing off. This gave Sally the feeling that he didn't fancy her any more. In fact, she even thought at one point that he was having an affair. What she didn't know, because he didn't discuss it with her, was that he was having health problems and finding it extremely painful to make love. Had he told her in the first place, she could have reassured him and they could have visited the doctor together to find out what the problem was. He didn't confide and it only came out in the middle of a huge argument when she accused him of not being interested in her any more. The fact is that embarrassing problems such as these are bound to happen at some time in a lifelong relationship. Sally ended up in tears and when Jim tried to comfort her, she admitted that she was losing confidence in their love and felt like he was pushing her away because she was unattractive to him. When he saw the damage that he was doing to his relationship, he confessed and very soon their relationship was back on track, with a little helpful advice from the doctor.

If you feel that something is wrong, talk to your partner about it. It doesn't make you less attractive. It doesn't make you any less of a person to be able to talk about things instead of pushing your loved one away because you are too embarrassed to talk. If you can't confide in your loved one, you need to learn to before it spoils your relationship.

Sara was afraid of lovemaking because of something very violent in her past. Ordinary lovemaking was okay but as soon as her husband started to explore different ways to make love, it brought back all of the bad memories. He didn't know he was pushing the wrong buttons and frequently the partner who does push the wrong buttons isn't doing so to cause their partner pain. When Sara opened up and explained things, he was able to adjust the way that he approached lovemaking and make all of those exotic positions possible without the connection between that bad event in her life and what was happening then and there. They built up a trust between them that allowed her to get beyond the problems of the past and start to trust life a little more and he was more compassionate toward her.

Talk about the things that worry you. If you don't like certain areas of your body to be touched because it causes you discomfort, explain it. At the same time, watch out for signs that there are problems with your partner and know what the wrong buttons are to press when you are in an intimate situation with him/her. This depth of knowledge about your partner helps you to build up a trust that will help you through future problems. It is worthwhile pursuing these problems and finding out what makes you feel that way. Your partner is exactly the right person to tell and to discuss the problem with.

Takeaways from this chapter:

The message contained in this chapter is clear. You need to avoid keeping things to yourself, particularly if they involve the interaction between your loved one and yourself. If you are able to discuss things with your loved one, he/she will have a better idea about the buttons that need to be avoided.

Belittling your partner does very little to his/her confidence levels and that's not the way to move forward. Remember that if you are worried about something happening in your relationship, such as getting the impression you are being pushed away, don't make assumptions. Discuss the problem and do in the following way:

1. There should be no hint of criticism in your approach.
2. You should never use comparisons
3. You need to understand that there may be health issues
4. You also need to understand that the buttons you are pushing may need to be changed. Not everyone likes the same things.

If you are able to explore your partner's body and let your partner explore yours, without any sense of anxiety, you are much more likely to enjoy each other's company. Talk about your problems rather than internalizing, because your partner can misinterpret your internal thinking. You cannot expect your partner to understand if you don't talk about things that matter to you.

Think of the laughter lines and how acceptable they are because other parts of your body are like that too. Each line is merely a sign of getting older. Wear them like medals instead of hiding them and being ashamed of whom you are. Of course, everyone has sensibilities. Share them with your partner so that your partner does not press the wrong buttons and misinterpret your response.

Chapter 21: Reconnecting Between the Sheets (Tantric Sex)

"Sex is like an atom bomb. A potent weapon which fascinates and frightens. We're afraid to let it loose, yet we all have our finger on the button."

Zeena Schreck

By the time you are about a decade into your marriage, the novelty of sex can wear off. The problem with most couples is that they either expect fireworks in bed or give up on intimacy altogether. The media does not help; they paint the picture of a fairytale love that transcends the physical boundaries of man and woman. Conversely, they also show passion of epic proportions between the sheets, even between an old man and woman who have grown beyond it. It's not realistic. When you consider the amount of abuse a body goes through in the course of a lifetime, it is more realistic to appreciate that you and your partner may need a little help along the way.

Neither end of the spectrum works. Passion between a married couple is important – couples with an active sex life definitely last longer than those who don't connect between the sheets. At the same time, you cannot let it define your entire marriage; sex can't be the only connection you make with your partner. You need to find somewhere in between these two extremes to keep your marriage happy.

The problem, then, lies in the routine monotony that lovemaking can quickly turn into. It becomes the marital version of *'wham, bam and thank-you ma'am'* that really does nothing to improve the intimacy between spouses. What you need to do is spruce up your sex life – try new things, do a little role-playing and explore a few kinks. I guarantee it will help you reignite the honeymoon phase passion.

Tantric sex, in this case, provides an excellent way of reconnecting with your partner. We have already discussed the books that are well known to illustrate and describe this kind of sex. As stated previously, they were written by Holy men to try and keep people's sex lives interesting, so that the couple not only experienced more sexual pleasure, but so that they also experienced a spiritual connection to one another. Too often, sex is just a physical aspect of a relationship and doesn't give you the spiritual connection you need as a human being. Conversely, your sex life becomes so boring you don't know how to express your love beyond the traditional activities in bed. In either case, tantric sex provides an excellent solution to both have fun times in bed as well connect spiritually with your partner. Before you do perform this type of sexual act, as mentioned before, make sure that you know the areas of the body that your partner does not like being massaged as you can spoil the moment by picking the wrong spot.

Eastern and exotic though it may sound, much of the tantric sexual practices are what any therapists would recommend to help improve intimacy between spouses. You will see for yourself what I mean when we go into detailed descriptions of these exercises. For now, try to understand the philosophy behind tantric sex – it advocates the exploration of the sexuality of the self in relation to the cosmos and the divinity.

The word *'sex'* itself comes with too many negative connotations; we have internalized this belief that pursuing pleasure and exploring our sexual belief is a rather hedonistic way of life and we need to stick to the traditional that is not taboo. So any new exploration in the bedroom is a half-hearted attempt to satisfy your own curiosity, rather than an emotional connection that brings both partners enormous pleasure.

Tantric sex believes that you attain a certain sense of enlightenment when you explore this sexual nature of your being; it makes sense, if you think about it. When you are confident in yourself and understand yourself fully, you are able to give more to your partner and thereby cement the connection with them in a way you weren't able to before.

The ultimate belief in tantric sex is the clichéd statement of *'it's not the destination itself, but the journey to it that matters.'* As used as this line is, it is a universal truth; when you take the time to enjoy every sensation and every interaction with your partner, you find your pleasure becoming tenfold and the levels of intimacy between you will also increase. Every sensory perception becomes magnified and improved.

We tend to categorize the idea of sex in a rather linear, progressive manner. In simple terms, it is the chasing of one's own orgasm through sexual stimulation. Tantric sex, however, advocates that as important as the orgasm is, the stimulation itself is an enjoyable process that should be experienced in full. In base terms – more foreplay, fun foreplay! When you follow the same sex script for years, you and partner get bored. When you spice it up with more fun things to do, even kissing can end up being absolutely exciting and arousing! Tantric sex also deals with problems such as premature ejaculation because you work toward making the climax last.

The reason why tantric sex works and why it builds intimacy between spouses is because it emphasizes feelings, rather than chasing an orgasm. There's no clear start of sex and there is no clear end. You experience an increased awareness of your partner, both physically and emotionally, and you connect more intimately than you ever have. Think of it in this way. It's the journey toward climax, rather than the destination – the actual climax – that makes tantric sex so pleasurable.

Climaxing in tantric sex can be a powerful thing; given that it is not the ultimate goal, it becomes an extra gift. You feel the *'full body orgasm'* – that mystical climax that every romance book talks about, instead of only feeling the high in your genitals region. It also allows you to become multi-orgasmic; women are naturally so, but our traditional perceptions of men's sexuality have denied them the chance to experience orgasms close together. For them, we believe ejaculation to be the ultimate climax; in reality, orgasm and ejaculation are two separate events that happen so close together that they seem to be one thing. There are practices in tantric sex that will allow men to try having *'dry orgasms'* – climaxing multiple times before ejaculating sperm. You can do further research into this online to increase your pleasure. For this book, we will stick to things that couples can do together to improve their intimacy.

Tantric sex echoes the *'live each moment to the fullest'* philosophy; stop worrying about how your partner is going to react or the family finances. Be fully present in the moment and allow the tension to build up. The whole point is to draw out the seduction and arousal period; the resultant prolonged orgasm you will achieve will be all the more pleasurable and mind-blowing. There is more to tantric sex than that, of course, but here is a step-by-step roadmap to get you started. You don't even have to call it tantric sex if it makes you uncomfortable or even follow up on further tantric sex practices. These steps are, in fact, just fun ways to spruce up your sex life overall and reconnect with your partner between the sheets. The activity is also very intimate and between you and your partner. It is something you share in common but that you share with no one else. Thus your intimacy levels rise and you are able to reconnect in a way that you would not normally be able to.

Create the Mood

Remember those days when you would take the time to make your partner a romantic candlelight dinner and then retreat to the bedroom to make soft, sweet love? Those days are not gone forever! You can recapture those moments by recreating them. Dim your bedroom and light up soft candles; spread soft flower petals on the bed to further the sensation of arousal and skin sliding against skin. The low lighting means that you can't see properly, so put all the other senses to good use and allow an element of thrill to be part of your lovemaking. Candlelight is also very sensual and if you are self conscious about your body, it will flatter you and only show off the curves!

Aromatherapy oils are an excellent way to begin. They smell amazing and an oil massage is one of the most arousing things to try in sex. When you touch, scent and feel your partner, you automatically become that much closer to them. Use silk – lingerie for women and silk sheets can add another sensual element to the whole experience. If you are going to use oils, get accustomed to having large towels in the bedroom that can be flung across the bed to soak up those oils!

Get Physical Slowly

When you go to bed together, don't jump in straight away. Start out slowly, with gentle kisses and cuddles. Dance for a while together – I don't mean tango or waltz this time. Just sway, pressing your bodies close together and try to relearn all those spots you haven't worshipped in ages. Let the tension build slowly; a strip tease is a perfectly fun thing to do at this time! If you have taken a shower together before going into the bedroom, drying each other's bodies and getting up close and personal at this time will help you to begin your journey into tantric sex.

The cardinal rule of tantric sex – *never look away from your partner's eyes.* It is not for nothing that the leads of a romance flick *'drown in each other's eyes.'* When you gaze into your partner's eyes, you increase the level of intimacy between you – your partner knows that you're here fully, giving them your whole attention and they allow themselves to be vulnerable to you in a way you haven't been in a long time.

Take your time with every touch. Don't rush to achieve a climax; when you feel like you're about to orgasm, step back, take a breather and then start over again slowly. Draw out your lovemaking – make sure the outside world doesn't intrude on this time together! Switch off all gadgets, place the kids with their aunts and uncles for the night and devote your whole attention to your partner. It will improve intimacy levels between you two like nothing ever has before.

Explore your partner's body. In the rush of things, particularly after kids, you probably haven't had the time to do more than simply stimulate the private places and do the deed in a quick, dirty manner. Now slow down, take your time and explore those nooks and crannies you've long since ignored. Arouse, tease and pleasure every erogenous zone, not just the private areas.

Be Kinky

Tantric sexuality is all about liberating you as an individual. In the traditional lovemaking score, men are the take-charge actors and women allow themselves to be the meek damsels in distress to be taken care of by their man. Tantric sex cancels out all that by taking away the idea of the orgasm itself; it is the *buildup* that's important. Seducing your partner, therefore, is vital and traditional seduction can get extremely boring within the first few tries. So what you need to do is to explore your own sexuality further and discover new kinks that you can practice.

One of the most fun, kinky and sexy things to do is to use a blindfold. Trust me when I say that this is an exercise that builds intimacy and trust between partners like nothing else. Allow your partner to tie you up and then blindfold you. You cannot see anything and, therefore, you have to put all your other senses to use in experiencing pleasure. Given that you can't see and you can't move, it can be a very humbling experience – you are vulnerable and at the mercy of your partner. It is an exercise in trust, and you need to have faith in your partner to have your pleasure foremost in his mind.

And when he/she pleasures you, you will find that your faith is not unfounded. The corollary of it is that your partner is humbled by the trust you place in him – he will feel vindicated of his decision to stay by your side and, in turn, allow you to tie him up or try something new, so that he can also be vulnerable in the manner you were prepared to be. This way, both partners are givers and receivers and by celebrating your sexualities and exploring kinks together, you build a new level of trust you didn't have before.

Practicing anal sex, particularly for the men, is something that can increase intimacy to an all-new height. Generally, between heterosexual couples, it is the women who get penetrated during sex. The traditional gender roles have ruined our understanding of human anatomy. In reality, the male penis *may* be the reproductive organ and it *may* give sexual pleasure, but anal sex can stimulate a man or woman far better and even allow them to climax in a way they have not experienced in the past.

This is because there is a tiny gland called the prostate that is accessible only via the male anus. The gland is walnut-sized and rests directly beneath the bladder – it is highly sensitive to stimulation and gives the male an enormous amount of pleasure. Using sex toys like dildos, along with lubricant, will allow them to attain new heights of ecstasy like never before. On an emotional note, that you're willing to let your wife – traditionally perceived to be the weaker and the one to be *'looked after'* – do this to you, you will let her know just how much you trust her and enjoy her. It will build an intimacy between you that you haven't ever experienced before.

But do keep in mind – kink exploration and discovering new things about your own sexuality *must* remain consensual and enjoyable. If you're uncomfortable with something, *let* your partner know. If you don't and they continue doing whatever they're doing to make you uncomfortable, you're only going to end up feeling resentful and angry and maybe even abused. Your partner can't read your mind – keep the communication open, honest and intimate. Try new things and figure out what works for you. Some couples, for instance, enjoy BDSM – if you don't, that's fine. Don't force yourself to fall into an expectation what you *should* find this pleasurable; that only leaves you tired and angry.

Your sex life is your own. You decide what works for you and what doesn't. You and your partner can have fun doing what you enjoy; don't be worried about whether it is taboo or whether it is strange. Trying strange things together can actually tie you together and bring you closer to one another. Conversely, your sex life doesn't *have* to be exotic – you don't have to follow anyone's rules to spruce it up but make it up as you go.

Did you know that the G spot, located inside the woman is more easily accessed via the anus? There are many women who do not climax. This is largely because the anatomy of a woman remains a mystery to men and they need to learn where the sensitive areas are. The clitoris is an obvious area of pleasure, but it is worthwhile exploring the inside of the vagina and working out where the G spot is during your massage of each other. A woman is entitled to have as much pleasure from the sexual experience as a man is.

Play with each other

Tantric sex – sex in general, actually – should be as fun as it is serious. The whole point is to enjoy yourself and connect intimately. To that extent, try to have fun when you make love. Tickle your partner – the sensations can be as sexually arousing as they are funny. Use your tongue, fingers and nails to tease your partner and arouse them into a state of desperation.

Role-playing can be a lot of fun in this instance. Perhaps your lovemaking has become boring and traditional; by pretending to be different people, you can recapture the excitement of discovering something new that has long since vanished. The pizza-man can seduce the babysitter or the teacher can punish the student for not completing homework – in any case, it is fun, it is arousing and it lets you rekindle the passion that has long since vanished.

One of the best ways to have fun in sex is to give each other massages and rubs. These are arousing and sensual, but they also help your partner understand that you appreciate them enough to work the tension out of their body. Conversely, by trusting you and letting themselves be vulnerable to you and your hands, they display faith and intimacy.

In tantric sex, there are two particular massages that are given extreme importance – *the Lingam Massage* and *the*

Yoni Massage, both of which are structured around increasing intimacy between couples. *Lingam* is the Sanskrit word for penis, and *Yoni* is the Sanskrit word for vagina. As the names suggest, the activity is a massaging of the privates, without chasing a climax or even sexual arousal. It is about feeling, understanding and appreciating your partner's body, thereby increasing the level of intimacy between you. Here is how you perform them. For the *Lingam Massage,* do the following (we'll use Deanna and Casper as an example again to make it easy to understand) –

- Casper lies on his back, with a pillow or a towel around his waist for support. His knees are spread apart to provide Deanna with easy access to his penis.
- Deanna pours a few drops of the aromatic oil onto her hands and rubs them together to warm it up. Now, she gently pours a few more drops directly onto the shaft of his penis and begins to massage his testicles.
- Deanna must make sure to change the speed, the direction and pressure regularly; she must also ensure that she doesn't cause any pain.
- If/when Casper seems to be about to ejaculate, she backs off and lets him soften a bit, before coming back to repeat the whole process.
- The massage ends with Casper deciding if he wants to ejaculate or not. When he is ready to stop, then Deanna stops. She covers him gently with her hands and allows him to relax and control his breathing.

Cardinal rule – *neither Deanna nor Casper choose to look away from each other during the whole process.* Their eye contact remains constant throughout, thereby increasing intimacy.

Deanna then chooses to allow Casper to give her the *Yoni Massage*, which is performed similarly –

- Deanna lies on her back, with pillows under her head and knees lightly bent to give Casper access to her vagina.
- Casper pours the oil onto her mound gently and on his hands, rubbing them to create soft heat. He then massages her outer lips, moving gradually inward to touch her inner lips.
- Casper must vary to pressure, the speed and the direction of his strokes – they must be deliberate and firm, but gentle.
- From there, he works his way up to the clitoris. He strokes, squeezes and plays with the clit using his left hand; simultaneously, he takes his right middle finger and tenderly inserts it into her opening and curls it backward towards his palm in a 'come here' gesture to stroke the G-spot.
- If Deanna is about to orgasm, he backs off and lets her breathe before continuing. The end is again, dictated by the receiving partner – Deanna – and when she is ready to stop, they stop. Casper places his hand on her mound gently and looks at her, letting her get her breath back.

Cardinal rule – *maintain eye contact. Do not look away at any time and be present in the moment fully.*

Both these massages let you understand and feel your lover's body in a way you have never before. They improve the trust, the intimacy between couples and shatter the traditional gender roles we have internalized over the years. They let you lean on one another and build on a faith that has always been there but never really used before now.

Cuddle

The last and perhaps the most important aspect of tantric sex – *post-coital cuddling*. If it is a cliché, it is only because it is true. When you hold each other and simply listen to each other's heartbeats, you realize just how lucky you are to have each other. You feel the *life* within you; you trust your partner enough to let go of your inhibitions and enjoy each other to the fullest.

Touch itself, without being sexual, has long been proven to increase intimacy between partners. We discussed this earlier, but I am reiterating it here to drive home the importance of it. When you feel like you want comfort or you need to reaffirm your connection with your spouse, don't be afraid to lean over and drop a kiss to their mouth or draw them in close and tuck them into your side. Intimacy improves just when you can do these small things – they are fueled by affection and not lust, and displaying that affection goes a long way in improving your relationship with each other.

Above all, remember – sex is important, but it is not the end of all things. Don't ignore it, don't push it to the last, but also don't let it dictate your entire relationship. Have a healthy sex life and try to be spontaneous and adventurous in the bedroom. Also remember – don't let the outside world dictate how, when and where you have sex. What you *should* do is a myth; do what feels right for *you* as a couple and try new things together. Your friends may enjoy one kink, but you don't need to! Appreciate yourselves as individuals and as a couple and focus on rebuilding your relationship instead of worrying about how you should be for the world.

I always have one set of rules for society and one for the bedroom and the bedroom is where you should be able to feel totally free to try that which is comfortable for both parties within a marriage. When you learn to give and take to this extent, you will find you look forward to bedtime. You look forward to rekindling that sexual closeness and that you won't worry about how your partner behaves behind closed doors or compare it with how other people behave. This is YOUR relationship. Make the most of it and enjoy each other. This partnership that you are in is for life, so why not make it the best that it can possibly be?

Takeaways from this chapter:

You are free, as a married couple to explore more exciting sexual activities. However, you do need to discuss this with your partner and make it something you both wish to explore. The Kama Sutra was written for the specific purpose of educating people about the spiritual connection that you can become aware of during tantric sex, and to help couples find the ultimate pleasure through their bedroom activities. Read it together if you want to, although there are some rather amusing and dated anecdotes within the text that may amuse you. Be aware that you are permitted to find some amusement in the bedroom as well as trying new exploration, but that this exploration has to be mutually acceptable. Never force your ideas upon your spouse if your spouse is unwilling or reluctant to try new things. Take it slowly, so that both of you are on the same acceptance level and are willing to enjoy each other without barriers being put in the way of that enjoyment.

The idea behind tantric sex:

1. That there is no limitation to your giving
2. That you explore more than mere orgasm
3. That you get to know your partner's sensitive areas
4. That you both get to control your orgasms to make the bliss last longer
5. That the end result should be a more spiritual connection between you as a couple.

This kind of sex isn't dirty, but you need to bear in mind that your upbringing will dictate how you see the sexual acts that you share with your partner. You need to remember that your partner may have inhibitions and slowly coax your partner so that you are able to work through the inhibitions, rather than assuming them to be dealt with. Total honesty with your partner is vital to enjoying this kind of sex. There should be no measurement of performance as that isn't what tantric sex is about. It's about total giving to one another, with very few limitations.

Chapter 22: Marriage – The Bottom Line

"You know it's never fifty-fifty in a marriage. It's always seventy-thirty, or sixty-forty. Someone falls in love first. Someone puts someone else up on a pedestal. Someone works very hard to keep things rolling smoothly; someone else sails along for the ride."

~ Jodie Picault

I introduced this chapter with this quotation intentionally. What the writer is saying is that marriage is never equal. There will always be someone who gets something more out of a given situation than someone else. However, with all the information in this book, you can even up the score and make your marriage work, reigniting the love that you feel for one another and keeping your marriage vibrant and happy. You are the only one who can assess the situation and decide if there is something that you need to do or to discuss with your partner to even up those odds. We have gone through a whole series of scenarios within the book that are common to many marriages but the bottom line is that if you are not happy in the marriage you are in, you need to address the problems that are making you unhappy and you may be contributing to those problems.

There is no one else that can do it for you and life is passing very quickly. Before you know it, if you are in an unsatisfactory marriage now, you will find that years have passed and that bad habits have become a way of life. You will have regrets that you didn't do anything earlier in your marriage to set things straight which is why it's important to tackle any discrepancies in the way you think marriage should be and the way your partner sees it. I watched my grandparents growing old together in a very unhappy marriage. They simply accepted that there was no way to change what had happened within their marriage, but in fact, there were many ways they could have improved it. My grandfather was a dominator. He thought that the little lady should stay at home and take care of his whims. Consequently, her life was put on hold. Her ambitions were thrown out of the window and by the time she reached the age of 78, she was ready to meet her maker because it was a delightful thought in comparison with having to spend another 30 years with my grandfather. So many marriages take this route. People are unhappy but too afraid to voice their opinions and it's time that you did and the sooner the better. Not only do you get a chance to rekindle your love affair with your partner, but you also get to show your partner that you are still the independent person that you always were, rather than an extension of your partner.

It's very hard to go through all of the changes that happen in a lifetime. You become someone's wife or husband and get that title. You then become someone's mother or father and somewhere along the line, you lose your identity. You may find yourself stuck in a marriage that doesn't excite you. You may find that your partner doesn't seem like the same person that he/she used to be. The fact is that the person you fell in love with has changed but, in a good marriage, the changes take place as an evolution of that marriage and strengthen the marriage rather than weaken it. If there is something that's bugging you now, try to imagine how it will bug you in 50 years because marriage is for a lifetime and can be a wonderful thing, once your ground rules are decided upon and you are heading in the same direction as your loved one.

If your sex life isn't that hot, it isn't just down to one person. There are two of you. Introduce new things that will excite you both. Try to experiment and spend more quality time with your partner even if you have kids. Let your partner know that his/her wishes come first, regardless of having kids invading your space. Let the kids go to their grandmother's for a weekend and shower each other with the kind of passion you always wanted to – without the problem of having to listen out for the tiny patter of feet.

The biggest hurdle to a happy marriage is in thinking that you are both an extension of each other rather than individuals. If your needs are not being met, you need to address this problem head on and discuss ways in which they can be met. A lifetime of being discontent is an awful long time. You have the opportunity now to have your voice heard and to adjust your lives so that they are the best that they can be for both of you. If you are indeed unhappy because of the pattern of your marriage, chances are that your partner isn't that happy either, so talking about the problems and ironing them out will help you to get back on track.

If you have ever reached that point when you see everyone else's marriage as being better than yours, you may have reached that plateau where the grass on the other side of the fence looks greener. It may have crossed your mind that being single again would be a great move, but believe me – the grass on the other side of the fence is the same color if you step into it because you make it what it is. In any relationship, new or old, the staleness of the relationship happens if you let it. What you need to learn is how to get over that plateau and move toward a happier place for both of you. It takes a lot of talking, negotiating and being honest about your dreams to get there. Perhaps your dreams, that you are hiding from your partner because you don't want to hurt him/her, are actually the same dreams as your partner has. You will never know until you talk about them.

There are all these standing jokes about married people and if you walk into a restaurant and look around you, you can usually tell the difference between the body language of lovers and the body language of people who have been together for years. I was in a restaurant not long back and the couple that came in said absolutely nothing to each other all the way through the meal. They had been married for years and had simply run out of things to say. If you want to liven up your marriage, show your partner the side of you that he/she has never seen before. Be unpredictable but make sure that your partner has sufficient trust in you to go along with the changes that you think would benefit your marriage. Listen to your partner. Talk about dreams, fantasies and realities and get back on the same page again. You may not think that it is possible, but with good will and love in your heart for your partner, it is indeed very possible.

Marriage

Janet and Keith were married for 35 years when their marriage hit the doldrums. Janet was no longer happy with the marriage and Keith was positively lethargic about it. What woke them up was the fact that they lost their close friends in a car accident. It kind of gave them a shock that made them look at their lives and appreciate everything that they had which they had taken for granted for so long. Janet recalls "I remember looking at Keith in the church at the funeral and thinking how selfish we had been. There was a look of silent understanding in his eyes because he saw it too." What they had lost in their marriage, they had lost because neither one of them made any effort any more. As soon as this wake-up call happened, Keith booked a cruise that Janet had always wanted to go on, and they began to re-ignite their love for each other, feeling lucky indeed that their marriage had survived all of those years and that they still had the same amount of affection for each other that they always had. They had simply put it aside for the more practical aspects of life.

"I had thought about leaving him," Janet confided, "but I didn't see anything else in life that would give me the same amount of satisfaction. It was my attitude to the marriage and his attitude that had made our marriage stale." The cruise did the trick but that could just as well have been a picnic under the stars or an outing to a nostalgic place. It doesn't matter how large or how small the gesture, as long as the gestures still happen and there is room for communication between you, there is always the possibility that you can get back what you started with, and find it better than before because you will both have matured and will be more capable of understanding that level of love that comes from a long term marriage.

Re-growing the connection between you is easier than you may imagine. It can begin with a shared memory that conjures up thoughts that are of a romantic nature. It can be something insignificant to someone else but something of great importance to you, as a couple. With the help of the advice contained within the chapters of this book, you now have a better idea of what it takes to keep your marriage alive. The small gestures that you make toward your partner count for a lot. You were once on the same wavelength, and those memories that you made together still count for something romantic in your lives. Let your partner know you remember them and don't be afraid of the changes you need to make to get your marriage back on track. They will have been worthy of your effort.

Takeaways from this chapter:

If you are looking for fault in your partner, turn that around and look at your own approach to your marriage because there is absolutely no doubt that you will have contributed to the unhappy situation you are now facing. Two people are in your marriage and voicing your dissatisfaction instead of addressing the problem in a calm manner may just be why your partner is edging away from you. So many people are unwilling to accept blame. Jessie and Ian went to a marriage counsellor. To all intents and purpose, Ian was the guilty party who was making the marriage miserable. Everyone had become involved. Jessie had criticized him to her parents, to his parents who had taken her side and to their friends. In doing so, the counsellor explained, she had betrayed his trust and the reason he wasn't being affectionate to her was because of that betrayal of trust. Thus, from this example, one can see that there are always two sides to the coin:

1. Don't discuss your marriage with others. Discuss it with your partner.
2. If you are unhappy, don't blame your partner for your unhappiness. Work it out together.
3. If your partner is lethargic in his/her approach to the marriage, look at your own actions to find out why and then do something to put the marriage back on track.
4. Remember that life is passing very quickly and regrets that you are building up inside you can make mountains out of molehills. If you have a problem, get it out of your system and stop using blame to justify your angry inner thoughts.

I used to think that people with unhappy marriages should divorce, but then I saw friends with marriages on the verge of divorce that had the potential to mend their marriages. The potential was something neither party could see, because they were too involved in the emotional turmoil of their marriages. If you do feel that a mediator would help you to get things back on track, approach your partner and let him/her know that you will do anything to save your marriage. Enlist your partner's help. Don't assume that you can deal with it by seeing a counsellor alone. This isn't just your marriage. Those who have done this found solutions together and were able to put the sparkle back into their relationships. Counselling helped them to see things in better perspective.

The bottom line is that marriage is the union of two people and there is no one better to examine problems at their base than these two people – before emotional turmoil sets in. Talking to your partner about dreams and hopes, sexual fantasies and fears allows your partner the freedom to express him/herself without worrying about the consequences of that explanation. Listen without judgement. Digest problems together and come up with solutions that work for both of you because your relationship can find a new sense of balance and become something very valuable once you drop all resentment and replace it with entire trust and affection. That's when you know that the struggle you have been through has been worth it and that the time that lies ahead is every bit as exciting as those first days of love and passion.

Chapter 23: Advice from People with Successful Marriages

"Happy is the man who finds a true friend, and far happier is he who finds that true friend in his wife."

– Franz Schubert

You may not have all of the answers to your dilemmas when it comes to marital harmony, although everyone likes to look at the stories of famous people and to use these people as role models. Of course, we also see famous people going through divorce and scandal, although those who are grounded and happy are also content to share the secrets of their relationships because they have found what it is that you are looking for – harmony and contentment.

Tom Hanks and Rita Wilson have been married since 1988. Theirs has been a happy marriage and they have also been through serious health issues together. Tom puts the success of his marriage to Rita down to actually liking each other. He also has a very humbling attitude in that he can't explain what his wife sees in him. I have used this as a great example of what a role model should be like. In this case, fame and fortune could have meant that Hanks was tempted out of wedlock had his relationship been less to his liking. Instead, he found that by sharing his problems and never hiding them, he and his wife enjoy a very stable and satisfying union. In fact, the relationship was so satisfying that he was able to describe his marriage as follows:

""I have been blessed beyond deserving. Since 1988, I have been happy in the warm embrace of a big, fat Greek family. I'm here because of my wife, Rita Wilson. She is the motivation of my best work. I wish everyone could share their life with as good a friend, a passionate lover, as close a partner, and as beautiful a woman as I have been able to with the mate of my soul, Rita Wilson."

You can see from this that the friendship between the couple is high on the list and that gives you the indication that you need to remember your partner is probably going to be the best and closest friend that you have in your life. He/she accepts all your quirks and still wakes up beside you every morning of your life. That's a true treasure and when you find your marriage hitting the doldrums, is something you need to remember. Rekindle that friendship. Ask yourself if you are treating your best friend in the manner a best friend deserves. You may be shocked at your answer, but it will help you to piece things together and to help bandage the wounds.

Sarah Jessica Parker and Matthew Broderick – Having been successfully married for over 20 years, you may be surprised at the advice given by this couple. They decided a long time ago that discussing their marriage with anyone was a no go area and that's good advice. Yes, of course, you may want to show off your husband or wife or let friends see how happy you are, but your dirty laundry is something that is not aired in public. When you look at stars, they are put in a terrible situation and are easily caught up in scandals when stories break in the newspapers about new liaisons or rifts within a relationship. However, if you translate their advice to your own marriage, you don't say bad things about your marriage to others. You don't talk about insecurities with other people. You turn to one another to talk about them. These are private things between a couple and Sarah Jessica Parker's quotation on marriage was short and sweet but very astute. "The secret is, we don't discuss it. With reporters, or anybody else." She also comes up with the conclusion that the success of their marriage is down to being able to talk a lot between themselves, opening up channels of communication that make them best friends.

Sean Connery and Micheline Roquebrune in 1973. Unlike his first marriage which was a marriage of opposites, this marriage was based on the fact that the two had so much in common and were such good friends. You may be seeing a pattern emerging here, but it is hoped that you will. The friendship element is what seems to be universal in successful marriages. In fact, Sean Connery said that he was thrilled that not only did his wife play and understand the game of golf, she actively encouraged him to play it.

There are thousands of successful marriages that you can use as role models, but the one thing that you can see is that friendship is vital to a happy marriage. If you are able to discuss things without letting emotions get in the way, you can improve your sex life, you can tackle problems and you are able to retain that sparkle in your relationship. In many of the cases interviewed for this book, the element of friendship played a huge part in successful compromise. If you lose that element of friendship, then this is a good starting point. This enables you to be free in your approach, to affirm your trust and love for your partner and to get onto the same level of thinking, so that nothing becomes too big a barrier to overcome.

Takeaways from this chapter:

The examples of marriages that have been used in this chapter have been used for the specific purpose of demonstrating that friendship and total trust between the two parties is what makes a marriage tick. These are celebrity examples, but there are examples that you can see in marriages that are successful in your everyday life. There are ways to improve the odds, but the best way to start the ball rolling is to first remember that you are your partner's best friend. If you are not, this is something you can work on because it is that level of friendship that allows you to open up all the avenues contained within this book so that your marriage becomes a very satisfying part of your life. The elements that you should always work toward are these:

1. Total trust in your partner
2. Expectation of trust from your partner
3. Understanding and embracing the differences between you
4. Enjoying the similarities you share
5. Cutting negativity out of the picture

6. Putting criticism behind you

When you can move forward in your life and re-establish that close friendship and bond you originally had with your partner, you are doing more than that. You are opening up avenues for exploration – whether that comes in the form of doing things together or of spicing up your love life. Friendship means you can laugh together. It means that you can be strong for one another at times when your partner shows weakness and expect their strength when you need it to help you get through a day.

Marriage is never going to be an easy ride. There are going to be difficulties that lie ahead, but the strength of your relationship dictates how hard those difficult moments are. Take time to listen as active listening means being interested in what is being said. Take time to cuddle and to show affection. When you do, you find that old feelings can show through the surface and that the love you felt for each other is still very much alive, even though it may appear to be a little mellower with age. Laugh at the same jokes, and if you don't understand the joke, laugh at your own ineptness once your partner has explained the joke. Laughing at yourself is part of the picture because when you can do that, you are also able to see the amusing side of life that keeps your marriage a fun place to be.

Friendship will guide you through bad times and good times and the special bond that you share with your partner allows that friendship to have no boundaries. It is this quiet acceptance of each other that makes a marriage into a very special place to be for both of you. This book was written with the specific intention to help you to find that friendship in each other that allows you to add new sparkle to every day that you share together. This may come in the form of recognizing joy in a child's eyes or recognizing sexual satisfaction and love reflected in your lover's eyes. It comes in the form of a bond or a sharing that is exclusive to you, as a couple.

Conclusion

Marriage, in essence, is a progress. It is filled with ups and downs and cannot be predicted. It cannot always be sunshine and roses, and it will not always be thorns and stones. Don't go into it with enormous expectations and don't give up at the slightest indication of trouble. There are times during the course of a marriage when you feel like you are not being listened to. There are yet other times when you don't give your partner the time to listen to his/her side of things. Slow down and enjoy it. Step away from any resentment you may bear and try to live in this moment in time, making it better than those that have passed and you can find mutual happiness.

Be willing to let go of your ego and try to be open and honest with your partner. Enjoy your partner's quirks. Don't hide your annoyance until it is too big to handle. Openly discuss problems and find solutions together. Don't buy into the myth of a fairytale marriage. It doesn't exist. What you need to buy into is total commitment to each other and total respect. Without that respect and trust, your relationship will flounder.

Have fun together and ultimately, allow yourselves to let loose and enjoy each other again. Responsibilities don't need to always get in the way – you don't have to *keep* worrying about the kids or the finances. Take time off for yourselves and try to spend time together, with each other so that you don't drift apart. Talk about your problems and listen to your partner's problems without interrupting. Come up with ideas that suit both of you and remember that marriage is something that you work on in small ways every day of your lives together.

At the end of the day, a marriage is about two people who want to make it work. Love is there; what is lacking is an expression of it. So don't be afraid to use those three magical words – both sets of them! *"I love you"* is as important as saying "Sorry" or "Please" or "Thank you". When you tell your partner that you love him/her, make sure that you also show your partner by the way that you behave toward him/her. Let your partner know you appreciate them and try new things together – you'll find that the love rebounds like never before and you're connecting in a way you haven't in years.

Try to avoid the clichés such as calling your wife "darling" in a generic kind of way. She may actually like it if you have a special name for her that you never call anyone else. Try to avoid assuming your husband likes sex in a certain position. Ask him. Talk about it and make the bedroom a fun place to be instead of simply somewhere where you sleep. For husbands who are looking for that extra special way to show their wives a little extra love, think back to the days of romance and you will find something that will remind your wife of the early days of passion. It isn't hard and you are still the same people. A look of encouragement or a smile of approval can go a long way toward making your marriage a great place to be.

Remember that marriage isn't just about convention. It's about walking the same path with someone that you have chosen and who has chosen you and learning to let the relationship evolve and grow as your likes and dislikes change and as you walk toward the twilight years together.

Marriage
Thank you for buying this book! I hope you found it useful!

BONUS

Visithttps://funnelb.leadpages.co/smarter-not-harder-business/ to get free eBooks, weekly tips, and the two free bonuses below when you join my free Ultra Book Club. Upgrade your personal and professional life today.

Free Bonuses:

- Top 10 Productivity Tips & Hacks: Guaranteed to Unlock MASSIVE Amounts of Time, CRUSH Decision Fatigue, and SKYROCKET Your Efficiency *and* Effectiveness .
  Visit https://funnelb.leadpages.co/smarter-not-harder-business/

- 23 Health Tips & Hacks to CRUSH Fatigue, Improve Sleep, Boost Sex Drive, and Heal Your Gut Visit https://funnelb.leadpages.co/health-tips-fatigue-sleep-sex/

CPSIA information can be obtained
at www.ICGtesting.com
Printed in the USA
BVOW06s2135181017
498106BV00009B/150/P